HOW TO WRITE AND SELL
TRAVEL ARTICLES

HOW TO WRITE AND SELL TRAVEL ARTICLES

Cathy Smith

ALLISON & BUSBY

First published in Great Britain in 1992 by
Allison & Busby
an imprint of Virgin Publishing Ltd
338 Ladbroke Grove
London W10 5AH

Copyright © Cathy Smith 1992

The moral right of the author has been asserted

ISBN 0 7490 0120 8

A catalogue record for this title is available from the British Library

Phototypeset by Intype, London
Printed and bound in Great Britain by
Mackays of Chatham, Lordswood, Kent

CONTENTS

This book is dedicated to my many friends scattered around the world.

PREFACE

Travel writing provides one of the largest markets for freelance writers. In almost every newspaper and magazine there is a travel section and most of the articles are written by freelance writers.

This book is directed at the inexperienced writer who wants to specialise in travel articles. It will also be useful for new writers of other non-fiction pieces, as some of the areas covered apply equally well to all types of non-fiction writing.

Although this book cannot guarantee sales, you will gain an understanding of what makes a good travel article, an appreciation of the importance of correct marketing, knowledge of how to get commissions, and how to present yourself and your work in the best possible manner.

1

TRAVEL WRITING – THE FIRST STEPS

There are tourists and there are travellers; we can all be tourists but not all of us can be travellers. A tourist is a sightseer, a statistic in the long queue outside Madame Tussaud's. A traveller looks beyond the obvious into what goes on in the streets and alleyways behind the famous facades, and wonders about the people – their customs and rituals, what they eat and how they spend their time. A tourist sends a postcard home, a traveller records his experience in a journal.

There's nothing wrong with being a tourist but if you want to be a travel writer you should also be a traveller. This book is written for those travellers and would-be travellers who long to put their experiences down on paper but don't know where or how to start.

Most beginners think they have to be accomplished writers in order to get published. This is not true. As an article-writing teacher I see writers of fairly modest ability succeed where more talented writers fail. Why? Because those who are successful have learned how to present their work in a professional manner, approach editors in an appropriate way and market their ideas with a view to *selling*.

Having gone through the pain of rejections, the stress of long hours spent working alone, and the anxiety of wondering if I would ever sell *anything*, I understand how beginners feel. Just remember that there is no magic formula. Travel writing, like any other kind of writing, requires perseverance and hard work in order to succeed. But if you apply yourself to the guidelines outlined in this book I'm sure it won't be long before you experience the thrill of seeing your first article in print.

Why be a travel writer?

If you are the kind of person who loves a challenge, is excited by new ideas and new faces, is flexible, adventurous and perceptive, you are probably halfway to being a travel writer already. If you find this description intimidating, don't worry – the more you travel and the more you write about your travels, the more confident you will become.

As a travel writer you will rarely be lonely and never bored. You will have opportunities to explore new places, meet interesting people, and learn new customs. And for this, you will also be paid. Is it then surprising that about thirty per cent of all students who enrol for article-writing courses want to write about travel?

The old cliché says that travel broadens the mind. It's true, it does. Writing about travel can enhance your life by providing you with a greater understanding of the world and its people. As you absorb new knowledge and meet people of different cultures you will gain a deeper understanding of yourself and your own culture. Travelling is easier for us than it was for our parents and grandparents and as a consequence we have become a more cosmopolitan society, and a better one for that.

As a travel writer you have a responsibility to your readers. Writing about your experiences allows you to share

them with people who will go where you have been; they
will see their destination through your eyes and will look to
you for truth and accuracy in hard facts as well as in things
more personal and subjective.

Everything worth doing in life carries with it a certain
amount of responsibility, but few occupations allow you the
flexibility, freedom and opportunity to indulge an adventurous spirit that travel writing does.

Even as a part-time travel writer you will enrich your life,
as well as your pocket. If you are the kind of person who
finds himself or herself reading a travel article and thinking,
'I could have written this,' you probably could. There's
nothing to stop you trying and even if you never publish
anything – but of course you will – your understanding of
the world will be enhanced by the process of writing about
your experiences.

Descartes said that 'Travelling is almost like talking with
men of other centuries.' Imagine if you could hop into a
time machine and spend a couple of weeks in seventeenth-
century Paris – there still are places in the world that have
changed little over the centuries and you can see them and
write about them.

What it takes

Like any other kind of writing, travel writing requires some
writing skill. This you can learn. Writing, like almost any
other craft, is learned by *doing*. The more you write the
more proficient you will become, but you will need more
than an ability to write. For instance, you need a spirit of
adventure which will spur you on to seek out the unusual,
to drive you along paths which have not already been worn
out by tourists' feet and by dozens of other travel writers.

It's too easy, and too safe, to eat at the restaurant 'where everybody goes' and which caters mainly for the tourist trade. Why not walk to the cantina or café at the end of the town and see what delicacies the locals are enjoying? You'll have more fun and probably meet some interesting characters. Not all your readers will fancy eating raw fish or fried witchetty grubs but your sense of adventure will enhance their enjoyment of your article.

Curiosity is a great asset to the travel writer; it pushes you around just one more bend in the road to see what's there, and makes you ask *who, what, where, when, how* and *why*. By being genuinely interested and asking questions, and by being a good listener, you can uncover wonderful gems of information about local history, learning anecdotes and stories about local characters, and places to visit that you may not have known about – all terrific stuff which will fill your article with life and colour. Don't be afraid to ask questions: most people are flattered to think you are seeking their opinion or advice, and as long as you are polite they are usually only too happy to oblige.

Energy and enthusiasm are essential if your travel stories are to be lively and interesting. It's no good writing about a street carnival in Mexico if all you did was stand on the side and observe. You need to get right in there with the dancers and experience the throb of the music and the excitement of the crowd swaying and pushing around you before you can describe to your readers what it is really like. If you are going to be a travel writer you cannot afford to be a passive tourist. Remember that you are paving the way for future visitors and you must use all your energy and enthusiasm to enjoy your experience to the full so that you can re-create it for your reader.

The world is a complex place and if you are to travel around it and write about it you must have a flexible attitude. Life would be boring if we were all the same, and part of the attraction of travel is the glimpse we get of diverse cultures, of different ways of doing things and other ways of viewing the world. We're all familiar with the stereotypical English tourist who wants chips with everything or the American who cannot live without a hot shower every day. Part of the charm of travel is to have new experiences, however strange they might be, so the next time you are offered a favoured delicacy such as a sheep's eye, swallow it quickly and think about what a good story it will make.

There is a market for *you*

Do you sometimes despair when you read travel articles about remote and exotic parts of the world that you know you will never get to? Take heart, for travel is not only about trips to outer Mongolia that cost the earth; you can sell a travel piece about almost any place providing it is of interest to the people who will be reading it. For instance, chosen at random from the magazines and newspapers on my shelves, I came up with the following: *Taste* offers a piece on Southwold in Essex, a traditional English seaside resort; *Bella* has an article on farm holidays in Britain; *Essentials* writes about Norfolk and Brighton; the *Guardian* has a feature on Constable Country. All of these places, and many like them, are holiday destinations for thousands of people each year and there are dozens of markets that take stories about them.

No matter where you live there is something of interest to write about if you look for it. Delve into the history of your village or town. Are there any connections with other countries? For example, the town of Washington in County Durham has connections with the ancestors of George Washington, the first President of the United States. An article about the area, how it is today, and what its links with George Washington are could very well sell to an American travel publication. Or perhaps there are unusual festivals which take place in your area and in which visitors might be interested. An example of this is a piece published in the *New York Times* travel section about a gooseberry competition which takes place in Egton Bridge, a village about forty miles north of York. Visitors love to read about off-beat events like this which are often easily accessible from the more obvious tourist centres.

No matter how ordinary your holiday destination seems, there is something to be written about it that will be of interest to some publication somewhere. Perhaps you have small children and are restricted to those places which lend themselves to family holidays. Write about them. Are the beaches clean and safe for children? Are there hotels which especially welcome children and provide extra facilities for them? Are there easy walks nearby which the whole family can enjoy? Perhaps there are working farms in the area which allow visitors?

If you like camping and have parked your tent in some unusual places, there are camping and walking magazines which take this kind of article. A friend of mine wrote a piece for the *Guardian* on the joys (and otherwise) of motorcycle touring in France.

If you enjoy travelling by train, write about it. It could be anything, from a short run on the Carlisle to Settle railway to something as grand as Paul Theroux's trip around South America which he wrote about in *The Old Patagonian Express*.

Perhaps you are the kind of person who likes to explore new places on foot, taking your time and poking around little streets and byways. There's lots of scope for such articles, especially with overseas magazines. Visitors often prefer to get off the well-worn tourist routes and they like to read about interesting buildings, historical facts and good places to stop for lunch which they can look out for en route. I sold a piece about strolling around Soho to an overseas magazine. I read up on the history of the area, walked around a few times in order to plan a route that would take in the most interesting points, and included a couple of nice pubs and places to stop for afternoon tea.

Anyone who has ever taken a writing course or read books on how to write will be aware of the command to 'write about what you know'. This also applies to travel writing. If what you know best is your home town or county, then write about that. It's amazing what you can discover with a little research in your local library. Whatever you write about, there's a market for it somewhere.

Being able to visit exotic locations does not necessarily give you more travel-writing opportunities than those who stay at home. Again, it's a matter of what you have to say. In general, people are becoming very sophisticated about foreign travel. It's cheaper than it used to be and we are venturing further afield in search of something different. But because a place is different it does not necessarily follow that it is easier to write an interesting article about it. It's as easy to turn out a cliché-ridden piece of writing about the Bushmen of the Kalahari as it is to write about the town you grew up in. Remember, almost any place can be grist for the travel writer's mill if it is looked at with a fresh eye and an enquiring mind.

Marketing – the beginner's nightmare

The importance of proper marketing cannot be stressed enough, yet it is something that new writers seem to want to avoid as much as possible. They prefer to write up their articles and then send them out to whatever publication takes their fancy, often without having first checked as to length, suitability of topic, style, or anything else. Very occasionally someone might be lucky and sell a piece, but for most people the all-too-frequent return of manuscripts, with the usual brief rejection slip, is a result of not giving some previous thought to marketing – to who their audience is and to the requirements of particular publications.

The different aspects of marketing are discussed in Chapters 5, 6 and 7 but I want to emphasise that you will greatly reduce your chances of being published if you do not take into account the requirements of the marketplace.

Successful travel articles are directed to particular audiences and you will get to know these audiences only by studying the magazines and newspapers they read. Many travellers never go any further then their armchairs – they like to share your experiences, imagine themselves alongside you as you brave foaming rapids in your flimsy canoe or trek through the Australian bush plagued by flies and mosquitos. They love to read about your adventure but they don't necessarily want to do it themselves, so you would not write a piece for this kind of reader which gives lots of facts on how to get there, how much it costs and so on. It's the atmosphere they want to share, not the actual journey.

On the other hand, many publications want travel articles which are destination-oriented. Their readers want practical information to assist them in making the same journey. If you sent an atmospheric piece to them it would be completely unsuitable and would very quickly land back on your doorstep.

If you have done some market study before you go on your trip and consequently have an idea of the kind of audiences you will be writing for, you stand a good chance of selling your material a number of times to different publications. For example, if you know ahead of time that you

TRAVEL WRITING – THE FIRST STEPS

are going to try for an outdoor activities magazine, a food
and drink magazine, a national newspaper that wants atmospheric pieces and a publication aimed at families with young
children, you will be on the lookout for things to write about
that will interest these audiences.

Proper marketing can help you in many ways. It not only
diminishes your chances of rejection, it can also bring you
regular work. Once an editor sees that you understand what
his readers want he will be more than likely to offer you
more writing assignments.

Opportunities galore!

You don't have to be an established travel writer to sell
your articles. Tourism and travel are big business and there
are hundreds of magazines and newspapers which take work
from writers who are unknown but who are able to produce
what they want. Every year new magazines come on to the
market, many of them with a travel piece or two on their
pages.

Numerous opportunities exist outside the obvious ones in
newspapers and general magazines. Anything to do with the
environment is hot news these days. If you have been to
the Galapagos or the Farne Islands, write about the birds
in their natural habitat, what is being done to protect them,
how easy/difficult it is to see them. Nature articles are popular and there are many outlets for them. Publications such
as *Green Magazine, BBC Wildlife Magazine, Birds*, and
Countryside are just a few that might be interested in what
you have to say.

If you are interested in walking you could write a piece
about how too many hikers are spoiling Britain's footpaths,
or perhaps about your experience in hiking with children.

Country Walking and *Great Outdoors* are two of a number of possible outlets. But you don't have to stick to the specialist magazines; such articles are of interest to the general reader too.

Favourite hikes or cycle routes which you enjoy but have not thought of writing about could make interesting articles. Readers enjoy hearing about other people's 'discoveries' and a piece like this might easily sell to a local newspaper. Newspaper and magazine editors will sometimes buy such pieces to complement larger articles on similar subjects. Don't be too proud to write small informative snippets of news – often these can give you an entrée to a publication.

News stories are of interest to the travel market too. Is there a splendid new hotel being built in your area? Find out more about it. Does it hope to attract tourists? If so, what does it have to offer? Perhaps there is a village or town near you that has been named prettiest or cleanest in the country.

You've always been interested in history? This is the perfect companion to travel writing. You probably love to potter around in the past, so why not write about some of the weird and wonderful information you have dug up – i.e. 'Ten things you may not know about Windsor Castle.'

Music lovers can write about festivals occurring in places like Edinburgh, Bayreuth, Provence, and many others. Tell the reader how easy it is to get tickets, describe the atmosphere, name the performers and, if you are able, try to interview a musician or two.

Combine your love of art with a travel piece. Describe your visit to Cezanne's studio in Aix en Provence, the Museum of Modern Art in New York, or the great art galleries of Florence. Many magazines take pieces like this.

Opportunities for the travel writer are everywhere; you just need to look for them. Inspect all the different specialist magazines which line the shelves of the main newsagents.

There are books for railway enthusiasts, golfers, sailors, hikers, mobile-home owners, cyclists, stamp collectors, anglers, skiers and many others.

Birth of a salesman/woman

Be prepared, as a beginning travel writer, to do your own selling. You won't always hit the jackpot with your articles but if you are persistent and refuse to allow yourself to be intimidated by rejection slips (more on these in Chapter 10) you will eventually begin to sell your work.

Think of the travelling salesman: he has to maintain an optimistic attitude; he must have confidence in his product; he needs to present himself in the best possible light; and he should know what he is talking about. This is how you should approach your travel-writing career. Have confidence in yourself and your abilities and be prepared to study the market place and approach as many publications as you can. In the beginning the rejection slips will probably rain down fast and furious, but one happy day you will sell something.

Like the travelling salesman, present yourself in the best possible way. When you write a query letter, or a covering letter to an editor, *never* say anything negative about yourself. If you have not published anything yet, don't tell the editor that. It is not relevant to the piece you are sending in, and if your work is good enough it will stand on its own feet. Don't tell editors that you are a beginning writer or that this is the first article you have ever sent out. It is not of interest and it won't help you.

Regard your travel article as a product which must appeal to the consumer. This means studying the market. Just as the travelling salesman would not try to sell his vacuum cleaner to someone who bought one six months ago, neither should you try to sell a piece on Corfu to a publication that has published something similar recently. It is important to think of your travel articles as marketable products and to approach the selling of them in a businesslike and professional manner.

Professionalism

Having determined that you will adopt a professional attitude to your writing, one obvious aspect of professionalism is that you should get paid for what you do. In the sports world, if you are not paid you are forever an amateur – no matter how good you are. The same holds true for writing. Often new writers are so anxious to get their work published they will write for nothing, or for very low-paying magazines. You should not do this. Remember what that old pro Dr Johnson said: 'No man but a blockhead ever wrote except for money.'

If your work is good enough to publish you should be paid a proper fee for it. It takes the same amount of research and writing to produce a piece for a high-paying publication as it does for a low-paying one, so why not aim high? If you have studied your market carefully and worked hard to produce the best piece of writing you can, there's no reason why you should not succeed. It may not happen right away, but if your standards are high and you stick with them you will begin to publish your work.

Professionalism also means developing productive work habits. Do everything possible to set aside a part of your house or flat as a work place. This is very important – this is where you will go to work, regularly. Don't wait until you are in the right kind of mood to write – remember that professional writers *write*.

Always present your work in a professional manner. Incorrect grammar, sloppy word choice, dull style, poor organisation and inadequate research are all signs of the amateur. It is not enough to have a good idea; you must be able to follow it up with a manuscript that looks professional in every way. You should *never* send in a handwritten manuscript, no matter how neatly you write. If you can't type I suggest you begin to learn immediately and in the meantime, if typing is a slow and agonising task which produces a messy manuscript, you might look to the services of a professional typist as a temporary answer to your problem. This can be expensive and is one of many reasons that, before you go to any unnecessary expense, you might wish to send the editor a query letter instead of submitting a complete manuscript. (Read about query letters in Chapter 7.) A professional travel writer has a strong grip of the skills of his craft, both in the basics of grammar and composition and the techniques needed to write non-fiction articles. All this you can learn. It just takes time and perseverance. If you are determined to approach your writing career in a professional manner you are already halfway to publication.

Chapter 7 deals with all you need to know about presenting your manuscript.

2

GETTING STARTED

The travel writer must have a keen sense of observation. Two people may be looking at the same view of the ocean, but one may see only a large stretch of water whereas the other will observe its colour and smell and will hear the sound as the waves slap on to the beach. If this person is a travel writer those observations will go immediately into his notebook.

Keeping a journal

The importance of keeping a journal cannot be emphasised enough. Your senses are most receptive when you see something for the first time. Unless you make a note of what strikes you as interesting and exciting you will lose that freshness of approach necessary to lift your writing out of the mundane and the predictable.

Beginning writers sometimes find it difficult to come up with a specific or original point of view or angle for their travel pieces. Chapter 4 deals with this in greater depth, but it is important to note here that frequently the point of view emerges only when you are actually on location. You cannot always tell ahead of time what your point of view will be and as you begin to explore an area and take note of what engages your senses it is more than likely that a specific angle will present itself. For example, if you are sitting at a street café in a popular holiday resort and a woman walks by carrying a basket of freshly baked bread, you might investigate where she bought the bread. Is it a small bakery tucked away in some corner where visitors don't go? If it is, you might get an interesting story from the people who run it. You could write a piece about a seemingly idyllic holiday spot as seen through the eyes of someone who lives there. Travel pieces don't always have to be full of praise; there is room for other points of view.

Your notebook should also be used for recording facts. Remember that readers and editors rely upon you for accuracy, so anything that you are not sure of should always be double-checked. Some travellers will take your article with them when they visit the place you have written about and your credibility will slump drastically if your information is incorrect. Don't take anything at face value. Facts taken from brochures can be wrong; information given to you by some local character can be misleading. Record in your journal only those things you have seen with your own eyes and facts that you know to be accurate.

Some beginning travel writers tend to wander around a place 'just soaking in the atmosphere'. This is fine for the holidaymaker but not for the person who wants to write saleable travel articles. Unless you record your impressions as you receive them, you will forget them. Yes, you may have an overall feeling about the place but you will have forgotten all those little things that will light up your piece. So do try to note details as you see them.

There are various ways of taking notes and you must find the method that best suits you. In his book *In Patagonia* Bruce Chatwin gives an example from his notebook which conveys something of his mood as he walks an endless road hoping for a truck to come by and pick him up:

> Walked all day and the next day. The road straight, grey, dusty and trafficless. The wind relentless, heading you off. Sometimes you heard a truck, you knew for certain it was a truck, but it was the wind. Or the noise of gears changing down, but that also was the wind. Sometimes the wind sounded like an unloaded truck banging over a bridge. Even if a truck had come up behind you wouldn't have heard it. And even if you'd been downwind, the wind would have drowned the engine . . .

That is a wind that the reader can really feel.

You may prefer to keep your notes brief, for example:
- black birds with red markings in the trees – find out name.
- soil is a dark red.
- orchids growing high in the trees.
- women walk by the river carrying washing on their heads.
- man sitting on wooden box eating strange spiky fruit – what is it?
- occasional patches of ground by river which are covered with butterflies.
- groves of banana trees – who do they belong to?

You can see that a picture begins to emerge.

Keeping a journal is an essential part of research and the business of gathering information becomes a habit after a while.

26

How to get ideas

Established travel writers and beginners alike are constantly searching for ideas that are fresh and interesting. This can seem like a daunting task but once you get into the habit of thinking about ideas, of looking for them wherever you go, of seeking them in your everyday life, you will realise that ideas are everywhere. There are probably many ideas in your immediate surroundings just waiting to be discovered. Is there a stately home, a good fishing river, or a splendid nature reserve nearby? Perhaps you live close to one of Britain's many long-distance walks? You could look for something of interest in your town that would tempt walkers to leave the track to visit it.

Read as much as you can. The travel sections in newspapers and magazines are full of interesting bits of information that could inspire ideas and a snippet mentioned in passing might provide the impetus for a whole article. Pick up brochures from Tourist Information Centres wherever you go. I visited Haworth, the home of the Brontë family, in West Yorkshire, and collected a number of leaflets from the information centre in the village. Not only was there a lot about Haworth, there were also brochures on the Yorkshire Sculpture Park and the fascinating little town of Saltaire – neither of which I knew anything about. I did visit them and both would make interesting articles.

Brochures from National Trust properties, famous gardens, ancient inns, are all sources for ideas and are full of useful information which can often be used in other articles.

Ideas can come at any time so remember to always carry your notebook with you. If you hear friends complaining, for instance, that Paris is too expensive, make a note of this. The next time you go to Paris you might want to investigate aspects of the city that are not so expensive and you could make this the theme of your article. I overheard some American tourists saying they didn't know where to go for afternoon tea. This gave me the idea for a piece on 'Teatime in London – The Best Places', which I have sold to publications in Germany and South Africa.

Travel exhibitions are goldmines for ideas. Every aspect of travel you can possibly imagine is on show and you can accumulate enough information to keep you going for months, if not years. There are brochures, photographs, maps, coach schedules, as well as information on tour operators, cruise lines, and anything else you can think of connected with travel. The World Travel Market is held at Olympia in London in early December and in January there is also the Holiday and Travel Fair at Birmingham's National Exhibition Centre.

Keep your antennae out for interesting and useful books which can inspire ideas. They don't have to be travel books. I have an eclectic mix, picked up in second-hand bookshops. A book by Michael Caine, *Not Many People Know That*, is full of weird and wonderful facts, many of which could trigger an idea for a travel article. For instance, some of the canals in Venice have traffic lights; until the end of the eighteenth century, lions were used to guard the Tower of London; and there are more than eight thousand elks in the woods of Moscow's 'Green Belt'. Don't those facts make you think?

If you are really stuck for an idea you could try thinking in terms of 'formula ideas'. These often work very well for popular markets. For example: What is the best . . . ?; Behind the scenes at the . . . ; The World's Biggest/Smallest/Best . . .

You can probably think of some of your own to add to the list. Try inserting relevant words like 'beach', 'hotel', 'train', 'ski resort', etc. You may not come up with an original idea but the method can be used as a device to get yourself thinking along the right lines.

Broaden your approach to ideas

Gain the most from your travelling by writing for as wide an audience as possible. For example, the requirements and interests of teenagers and retired people are usually quite different, as are those of single people and parents of young children. Keep your mind open when looking for ideas and make a note of anything you notice that might appeal to a particular group of people.

Don't forget about audiences with particular interests and hobbies. If you chance upon an area full of interesting antique shops, there are a number of antiques magazines that might be interested. Fishermen on holiday are always looking for good spots to cast their lines, so don't forget about the fishing magazines if you hear about a lake or stream off the beaten track that would delight their readers. Gardening, photography, and food magazines are all prospective markets for your articles, so do try to collect as wide a range of ideas as possible when you are on your trip.

Keeping track of your ideas

Unless you make some effort to organise your material you will get into a dreadful mess. All those brochures you collected, the newspaper clippings you tore out and the notes scribbled on bits of paper when you didn't have your notebook with you need to be in some kind of order so that you can easily retrieve them when needed.

Most freelance writers keep an ideas file. How you set up your files depends on you. You could have files for each individual country or place you are interested in or you could have a file for each individual idea. I favour the latter. For an article I wrote on stately homes, for instance, I put into my file information from National Trust brochures, rail schedules, historical information I had got from the library, details of organised coach tours, and anything else that was relevant.

You will, after a while, become an information gatherer, especially once you have a number of ideas files on the go. Everything you read will be scanned for snippets to put into your files. Even if the information you gather is not all directly relevant to the point of view you have in mind, collect it anyway. You'll find that a fat ideas file is a valuable source for many articles, not just the one you happen to be working on at present.

I keep files of newspaper clippings which are useful for giving me an overview of what kind of piece the editors are interested in. They are also a good source of ideas and you have on hand the information that gave you the idea in the first place. I file the clippings loosely under countries and whenever I go to a new place I go through them and take out whatever may be of use to me.

Another advantage of keeping ideas files is that some good articles can come out of combining ideas. For example, let's suppose you would like to write a piece about a walking holiday in Normandy and you come across an article in a magazine describing a cycling tour of that area. The combination of these two approaches might give you a more unusual article.

Later, when you have more confidence and are thinking of approaching editors with suggestions for articles, you will find it pays off to have a healthy collection of ideas files. If you can give an editor two or three good ideas you will make a good impression. Editors tend to give work to people who they can trust to come up with lots of good ideas. Ways of approaching editors are discussed at length in Chapter 7.

How to work efficiently

Most people who have to go out to a job every day would not think of asking themselves whether or not they feel like going to work. Very often they don't feel like it, but they go anyway; if they didn't they would not keep their job for very long. Yet, one frequently comes across beginning writers who say 'I can only work when I'm in the mood'. Professional writers do not wait for the muse to come. What if she never arrives? The serious writer gets down to the job whether he or she feels like it or not.

One of the most important things you can do to help yourself along the road to being a pro is to find a workspace that is your own, not one that is shared with other members of the family. While this is not always easy, with a little ingenuity you will probably be able to come up with something. Why not use a corner of your bedroom as a writing place? All you need to begin with is a small desk or table where you can leave material that you are working on, a few shelves for your reference books, and a typewriter or word processor (more about equipment later). If you share your bedroom with someone and are continually being interrupted, perhaps you could set up your space in the garden shed, the attic, or even a large broom closet. Privacy is more important than a large space and using the same place every time you write helps you to establish a routine that will encourage you to write regularly.

Of course there are writers who can produce excellent work at the kitchen table, with noisy children running around, spouses on the telephone, or the television blaring in the background, but these are the exception. Most of us need some peace and quiet to allow us to think.

Once you have your own workspace, plan a routine that suits you. If you have a full-time job and are trying to fit in time for your writing you will obviously have to choose between mornings and evenings during the week. If you are not a 'morning person' don't try to force yourself to stagger out of bed any earlier than you have to in order to get in a spell of writing before you go to work. It will probably make you very grumpy and take away any pleasure you may get from writing. Find the time that suits you best. If you are too busy or too tired to write during the week, put aside a few hours each weekend and try to keep to this routine. Make this your 'writing time', which other family members should respect and leave you alone to get on with it. Routine is very important and a regular routine means that writing becomes a normal part of your life. A good work routine is a mark of the professional.

How you organise your working procedure is up to you and there is no hard and fast way that is better than any other. However you decide to do it, make sure it is efficient. It's very frustrating if your files are disorganised and you cannot put your hand on information when you need it. I have a four-drawer metal filing cabinet; one drawer is for idea files which I initially list under fairly general titles of countries or places. Within each 'place' file I have individual ideas, each in its own plastic folder. For example, in a file marked 'Amsterdam' I have plastic folders labelled 'Amsterdam's Brown Cafés', 'Canal Walks', and one marked 'Amsterdam – Miscellaneous' into which goes any snippet I come across that is to do with Amsterdam. This is very useful for generating new ideas. Another drawer is for published work and I keep adding more information to these files as I may want to write another article on the same place at some later date and any new information I have in the file will be very useful. Another drawer is for business stuff like receipts, accounting, insurance, etc. And the last drawer is for miscellaneous bits and pieces, such as files on places I have never visited but would like to and would perhaps also like to write about.

Have your magazines organised in such a manner that you can quickly retrieve information when you want it. Many writers keep a card index filed by topic. For example, if there is an interesting article in *Good Housekeeping* on Majorca you could mark the name of the magazine on an index card headed 'Majorca' and give brief details of the piece and the date of the magazine. Travel writers, like all other journalists, use material that other people have written – not to plagiarise but rather as a source of tips on what to see, costs, etc. All of which, needless to say, you must verify yourself.

Rather than use a card index, I prefer to clip any articles that interest me and file them in the appropriate idea file. Many writers dislike cutting up magazines, but this means you can end up with masses of publications on your shelves which you need to keep as they are referenced in your card file. My method enables me to throw out magazines when I have taken from them what I need. Choose a method that suits your temperament and method of working.

The proper equipment is also important in helping you to work efficiently. Of course you must have a typewriter. Manual typewriters are fine up to a point but they are more tiring to use than electric ones and if you are not an expert typist it shows – the key pressure is uneven and mistakes are less easily disguised. Many writers who have moved on to word processors sell off their electric typewriters; you could buy one very reasonably.

And what about word processors? I would suggest that you wait a while before investing in one of these wonderful machines. The word processor is an invaluable tool and can speed up a writer's production enormously, but it will not make you a better writer. Many established writers refuse to go near them, fearing that using high technology will impair their creativity. Most writers, however, find that once they have used a word processor they can't imagine life without one. Chapter 10 deals with word processors in greater detail.

Tips to get you going

Now you have your workspace and working routine set up there is one thing that you need above all in order to become a professional: discipline. Don't allow yourself the luxury of even thinking about whether you feel like writing. Sit down and do it. There are various techniques you can use to help you over those difficult moments when all thought and imagination seems to have fled and the blank page sits accusingly in the typewriter.

Your can begin by doing something that is related to writing, perhaps by going over a piece you have written previously. Look at it with an editorial eye. Could it be improved? Mark any changes in pencil, make notes in the margin. Let your writer's mind take over those thoughts that are blocking you from writing. At the very least, this will get you thinking about the process of writing which is the gear you need to be in to get going.

Another device which may help is to write your article as if you are writing a letter to a friend. This can often help to loosen up your thoughts since you will not be paralysed by the idea that it is for publication.

I often browse through books on writing or travel articles that I have collected. Anthologies of travel writing, like *The*

Best of Sunday Times Travel, can also be helpful, as well as acting as triggers for new ideas.

If you really do have trouble in motivating yourself you might want to ask yourself why it is that you want to write. It can be helpful to clarify your thoughts in this way. Perhaps you feel a burning desire to write, to express all the things you have seen and done? Is it a way to earn a little extra money or do you want the satisfaction of seeing your work in print? It can be useful to look at what your motivation really is. When you are clear about what you want and why you want it you are more likely to try that little bit harder.

Dealing with writer's block

Gene Fowler said 'Writing is easy; all you do is sit staring at a blank sheet of paper until the drops of blood form on your forehead.' I'm not suggesting you go to such lengths, but if in spite of all your efforts, you are still suffering from a horrendous case of writer's block, what else can you do about it? One of the best ways I know of is just to write – get it down on paper in any shape or form. If you are trying to write a piece about your trip to Florence write down anything that comes into your head – let yourself think randomly. Even if what you write down is not directly connected with Florence, don't let that interrupt you. What will emerge from this effort is a lot of words, many of which you may not use. But at least you are *writing* and even if you have to throw it all away you have broken down the barrier between mind and hand which was stopping you from doing anything. Professional writers say, 'Don't get it right, get it written.'

Very often the cause of writer's block is nothing to do with writing itself but rather to do with other things going on in the writer's life which prevent him or her from concentrating on the business of writing. If you feel tired and your concentration is zero, perhaps you have been working too hard at other things, such as your day job, your children, your housework. If you really are tired, don't force yourself to write. Take a few days off and try to relax and catch up on your sleep. You will come back to the typewriter fresh and more able to concentrate.

If you are trying to write for a living and finances are troubling you, perhaps you should take a part-time job for a couple of days a week in order to bring in some regular money. The pressure of having to earn can be a real block to creativity.

Take a look at the subject you are trying to write about. If it is something you are not really interested in, perhaps you should deal with it later and concentrate now on something that does interest you. If you have a commission to write a piece about a trip you took on a cruise ship and you were bored during every minute of it, that's hardly a topic to tackle when you are feeling less than at your peak of creativity. Put it aside for a day or so – few deadlines are so rigid that you can't do this.

Remember that every writer faces writer's block at some point. The difference between the professional and the amateur is that the professional *forces* herself to write, whereas the amateur often gives up all too easily. Write regularly and have a few tricks up your sleeve to help you get going whenever you feel blocked.

3

GETTING INFORMATION

Research is the backbone of most non-fiction writing and travel writing is no exception. Readers expect to be provided with correct information so it is important for you as a travel writer thoroughly to research your destination.

Research before you go

There are many advantages to doing some research before you go and the good travel writer learns to plan ahead. Research can help you decide on a particular destination. You may be longing to see Greece and to write about it, but how do you decide which part to visit? Unless you have a definite commission to write a piece on a particular place, you are going to have to spend some time with guide books and maps until you make up your mind. Research not only helps you decide where to go, it also tells you the best way to get there, what to see, where to stay and where to eat; so it makes sense to gather a good part of this information before you leave. Of course there is much that you cannot research ahead of time, and would not want to. You need to be open to unexpected new sights and experiences.

When you arrive at your destination you will, with some

pre-trip research, have an idea of what it is you want to see, some understanding of the culture and how to avoid doing things that upset people. For example, in some countries people are offended if you take photographs of them, in others gestures that are acceptable in our society are considered very rude. Make sure you know something about the politics, history, climate, food and dress. It doesn't take a great deal of effort to find out about things like this before you leave. You might find it useful to take your notes with you.

Researching your destination ahead of time can help you define your angle. If there is a rare colony of birds on your Greek island you may wish to build an article around that. Or perhaps the cuisine is unique or there are marvellous walks. You will also save yourself time as you will have decided ahead what it is you want to see and what kind of questions you want to ask.

If you don't do some advance preparation you might easily miss something important. It could be very frustrating to find out when you get home that there were some historic ruins only a bus ride from the village where you were staying. When your article is published there's bound to be someone who will write in to ask why such important ruins were not even mentioned. Guide books cannot always be relied upon to tell you everything, so the more you can find out from various sources before you leave, the less likely you will be to miss something significant.

Plan well ahead for special anniversaries. Find out which city is to be chosen as the European City of Culture, as Dublin was for 1991. Are there world fairs to be held, like the one in Seville in 1992? If you are going to be away during Easter or Christmas, find out if there are going to be any particular celebrations during your stay. This kind of research frequently gives you ideas for a strong angle for your article, and can help you to produce an interesting and descriptive query letter which, in turn, may bring you a commission before you go. (Query letters are discussed in Chapter 7.)

Don't worry about accumulating too much information – it's better than having too little. You will be able to take from it what you need, rather than being forced to use whatever is at hand at the time of writing the article.

Research facilities

Before you can begin to accumulate information you have to know where to find it and the obvious first stop is the library. If you have access to a good reference library so much the better, but even the smallest local branch library will have a travel section and this is as good a place as any to begin your research. I like to begin with the various travel guides. Browsing through a few of these can give you a good overall view of what there is to see and they all seem to have their own emphasis. Some have very good maps but the information is short and scrappy. Others give better historical background information than others, and some report on night life – where the best clubs and discos are, for instance – whereas others never mention this aspect. Have a look at a few guides and take from them what is most useful for your particular approach.

My next step is to visit the reference library and spend an hour or so with the *Times Index*. The *Index* is published monthly and is bound into volumes which are on the open shelves of the library. Everything that has been written in *The Times* from 1790 to the present day is noted in these indexes. If, for instance, you wanted to check on any articles that may have been written during the past five years on, say, Crete, you simply look up 'Crete', note the references and ask the librarian for copies of the appropriate edition. Many reference libraries now have all their newspapers on microfiche and also provide the necessary equipment for you to view it. It's helpful to see what has been written about Crete by other travel writers, and they may mention aspects that you would not find in a travel guide. It may be that nothing has been written in *The Times* about Crete. In that case, *The Times* may be a possible market for your article. The *Guardian* also has an index which goes back to 1986.

Of course there are many other newspapers which publish travel articles. If you live in or close to London, the British Library Newspaper Library in Colindale has the major holding of newspapers and weeklies in the United Kingdom. The contents of the newspapers are not indexed by subject so I'm not sure how helpful this library would be to you as a travel writer unless you knew of a particular edition which contained an article you wanted to see. But if there is a piece that you really need to track down, this is the place to do it.

If you are concentrating on the historical aspects of a place, you should read some books on history, mythology, art or anything else that will give you a picture of the past.

Other sources of information are atlases and encyclopedias. The *Encyclopedia Britannica* has signed articles, which means you can find out who wrote them, and if you look up their name in the card index file you may find they have written books on the subject you are researching. Remember to do research on your subject, *not* your idea.

Check out geographical dictionaries, gazetteers of the world, books of facts, and anything else that may help you. Learn how to use your library and if in doubt ask the librarian.

Other sources

A few hours spent in the library will get you started with your research, but there are many other sources to tap for information. If you are writing a piece about the area you live in, don't forget your local newspaper. They may have a clippings library which you can use. Look back at old editions; they might provide you with useful historical information or anecdotes you can use in your travel article.

You should also read at least one Sunday newspaper with a good travel section. Many daily newspapers produce a weekend magazine which contains travel articles and I also recommend that you read a daily paper regularly. Travel writers should know what is happening in the world.

Travel agents can be a mine of information. Not only do they stock lots of brochures, they can be very helpful with specific queries. If you are staying in a particular hotel, ask your travel agent where exactly it is situated. If it is too far from the centre of things you could waste a lot of time getting to and fro. If you plan to take a sight-seeing tour while on your trip, ask the travel agent which is the best one, how much it costs, is it in English?

I have found consulates very helpful as well. If you are not sure of the meaning of a particular festival, want to know about their national day or need the proper title of their ruler, these are the people to contact. In some instances they are able to lend you photographs or transparencies to use with your article. You would, of course, have to give the photo credit to the consulate, but if you don't have good pictures of your own or your camera stopped working while you were on your trip, the pictures you borrow from the consulate can help make your article more saleable.

Collect in-flight magazines when you travel by air. They are a good source of information as well as being a possible target market. Ask friends to bring them back for you when they travel.

As you write more pieces you may find you like to focus more sharply on very specific aspects of travelling. You might, for instance, be interested in writing about food, camping, animals or birds, music. The possibilities are endless. Collect magazines that are in any way connected with your interests. The more background information you have the better.

Help from other writers

Other writers can be a good source of information and inspiration. Jan Morris, in an essay written for *Rolling Stone* magazine, describes her impression of Washington, D.C. as follows:

From the center of that allegoric cemetery one may look out across the Potomac to the grand sweep of the capital beyond. Nothing could appear much less American, for while America is above all a country of verticals, artistic, economic, symbolic, phallic, imposed splendidly upon the passive landscape, Washington, D.C., is all horizontal. Nowhere is much flatter than Washington. The ground is flat. The style is flat. The architecture is deliberately flat. From up there in the Arlington cemetery the whole city seems to lie in a single plane, without depth or perspective, its layered strips of blue, green and white broken only by the obelisk of the Washington Monument and the Capitol dome, as the massed ranks of Arlington are interrupted only by the graves of specially important corpses. It looks like a city of slabs, reverently disposed, and only

the jets from the National Airport, straining themselves
with difficulty out of the *ambiance*, throw a bold diag-
onal across the scene.

How observant she is! She has looked at Washington with
the eye of an artist, noting shapes and colours and putting
them together with words to create a vivid canvas.

By reading other travel writers you can broaden your
approach to your own writing and can pick up information
at the same time. Read with a writer's eye. Make note of
any information that may be of use to you and passages you
like, and file for future use.

Many of the great classic writers are a source of information for the travel writer. Study their descriptive passages
and try to make your own as rich and as interesting as
possible.

You would not describe Joseph Conrad as a travel writer,
yet his writings about mysterious tropical shores and the
grandeur of the sea are some of the best descriptive travel
writing I have ever read. In his story *The Lagoon*, he writes
as follows:

The forests, somber and dull, stood motionless and
silent on each side of the broad stream. At the foot of
big, towering trees, trunkless nipa palms rose from the
mud of the bank, in bunches of leaves enormous and
heavy, that hung unstirring over the brown swirl of
eddies. In the stillness of the air every tree, every leaf,
every bough, every tendril of creeper and every petal
of minute blossoms seemed to have been bewitched
into an immobility perfect and final.

John Steinbeck is another wonderful writer from whom we
can learn to observe with a writer's eye. Look at the opening
passage of *Cannery Row:*

Cannery Row in Monterey in California is a poem, a stink, a grating noise, a quality of light, a tone, a habit, a nostalgia, a dream. Cannery Row is the gathered and scattered, tin and iron and rust and splintered wood, chipped pavement and weedy lots and junk heaps, sardine canneries or corrugated iron, honky-tonks, restaurants and whorehouses, and little crowded groceries, and laboratories and flop-houses . . .

Read Edna O'Brien for the flavour of Ireland and Paul Bowles for a taste of Morocco. There are many other writers you can turn to for examples of what the people and the landscape are like. Use them to help you on your own journey as a travel writer.

There are many markets for your work. Some will require straightforward, factual articles, others will want lyrically descriptive pieces, and some will want a combination of the two. Read anything you can get your hands on that will improve your knowledge and your writing.

Accuracy

I mentioned in Chapter 2 the importance of recording facts in your journal. Readers and editors rely upon you for correct information and not only should you be careful about getting the facts right in the first place, you should also double-check them before you send off your article. Don't assume that everything will be same as it was three months previously. Prices change, train and bus schedules alter and restaurants go out of business, so it is very important to check your information and produce an article that is as up to date as possible. A good plan is to check more than one source in order to avoid inaccuracies. And always make a note of the source of your information.

Be precise in the way you give information. For example, if you use expressions in your piece like 'The ruins are only a short walk from the village,' tell the reader exactly how far it is. A short walk for one person can seem very long to another. 'A half day's drive' can mean anything from twenty to a hundred miles, depending on how quickly you want to reach your destination. If you have written about a nearby town that sells reasonably priced, good-quality handbags, tell the reader exactly what they cost. If you don't record facts such as this while you are on the spot you will inevitably forget and it is not always easy to get such information once you are back home.

It is not difficult to be accurate. As long as you remember to double-check your facts and be as honest as possible, you should not run into problems. Of course, disasters can happen. If you have recommended a particular cruise and the company decides to cancel it the week your article appears in print there's not much you can do about it. But if you have done your best to present a piece that is as up to date and accurate as possible, the editor will be aware of this and will not attach any blame to you.

Build your own reference library

Although books are expensive I would strongly advise you to start building up your own reference library. It is not practical to have to run to the library every time you want to know something and there are a number of basic reference books that you should have at home to dip into whenever necessary.

Apart from a good dictionary, other books worth owning

45

are *Writers' & Artists' Yearbook* and/or *The Writer's Handbook*. Both of these are published annually and contain invaluable information on potential markets for your travel articles. They also contain short articles by professional writers which are very helpful. In the 1991 edition of *Writers' & Artists' Yearbook*, for instance, there is a piece on 'Writing for the European Community' by Barbara Wood-Kaczmar, which describes the new opportunities opening up for writers in the huge European market of over 300 million people.

If you have used the same word a number of times and have a mental block about an alternative, a book you should have on your shelf is *Roget's Thesaurus*. A thesaurus helps you decide upon the exact word you want. If you find clichés, like *awesome* for instance, come to mind all too often, Roget offers the following alternatives: *wonderful, wondrous, surprising, astonishing, amazing, astounding, startling, stunning, unexpected*, and many more.

Ann Hoffmann's *Research for Writers* is a most useful book which helps you to find your way around the library and includes information on methods, sources and specialist libraries.

As a travel writer, atlases and gazetteers are helpful. *The Times Concise Atlas of the World* takes up a lot of room but has a very comprehensive gazetteer-index, and a good atlas is the *A–Z Great Britain Road Atlas*.

There are many good books on grammar and English usage. One of the best is Fowler's *Modern English Usage*, and another that I have found to be very good is an American publication called *The Elements of Style* (Strunk and White).

A guide to dates and anniversaries is a boon to the travel writer who is blocked for ideas. I have *Chamber's Dictionary of Dates* and it has provided me with a number of ideas for travel articles. For instance, included in the list of events which occurred on 8 November I found the following: in 1974, after 300 years in central London, Covent Garden market moved to its new site at Nine Elms. Not much information, perhaps, but enough to give me an idea for a piece on Covent Garden which I subsequently sold.

I like to collect books that have anything at all to do with travel and on my shelves I have a mixture picked up at jumble sales and Oxfam shops, as well as from the travel sections of bookshops. Each year I buy *The Best of Sunday Times Travel* which contains winning entries from the annual travel-writing competition offered by *The Sunday Times*. They make fascinating reading and many are written by beginning writers.

The Sophisticated Traveller series contains travel articles which have all appeared in the *New York Times*. Although originally written for an American readership the contributors are well-known writers from around the world. I have three books from this fascinating series, which contain articles from writers as diverse as Alberto Moravia, Muriel Spark, V. S. Pritchett and P. D. James. Snap these books up whenever you find them.

The Good Food Guide is useful for discovering good places to eat in Britain. Depending upon the kind of article you are writing, readers often like to know about good restaurants in the areas they are visiting.

Great Walks of Britain gives directions, detailed maps and a description of features en route for 38 walks and I have used it often for information and ideas. Other similar publications are available. I have books on English gardens, National Trust properties and the London bus and Tube system. All are well used.

You will need a magazine library too, to study the markets and see what is going on in the travel-writing world. How to choose target magazines is discussed in Chapter 5 but you should collect magazines that take travel articles whenever and wherever you can.

Collect the in-flight magazines whenever you fly. If you visit English-speaking countries, buy travel magazines to see what they are interested in. Buy British travel magazines too, and large hotels which are part of a chain often have their own magazines which contain travel pieces.

Build up your library with any kind of book or publication that interests you and that can help you with your travel writing.

4

GETTING IT RIGHT

Never be tempted to drop an idea because some well-meaning friend tells you it's been done before. There are few places that have not been explored and written about, and those that have escaped are generally in some remote part of the world that most people could not afford to visit in any case.

Writing about well-worn destinations

It's true that many places have been done to death but even the most tired of destinations can be revived if looked at with a fresh eye and a willingness to explore aspects that are not obvious. It's no good suggesting to an editor that you write something on Provence. You will be asked, somewhat wearily, what exactly you have in mind. If you instead suggest something like 'Walking the Hills of Provence' or 'Cezanne's Provence', you will have a much better chance of getting a commission, and at the same time the editor will see that you are a person who can come up with ideas.

If you are visiting a place that you know has been written up many times and you are planning to write an article, read as much as you can about your destination before you leave. Most guide books give the same basic information but I have found that there is usually some small fact contained within their pages that surprises. This can often become the focus of an article. Look for the unexpected little titbit and see if it is something on which you can hinge your article. For example, I read somewhere that Milan cathedral took almost six hundred years to build. Perhaps a piece entitled 'Milan Yesterday and Today' would be interesting, with the cathedral – the onlooker throughout the centuries – as the focus.

Travelling by unusual means of transport puts a whole different slant on a well-known country. If you have cycled around France, write a piece from the point of view of the cyclist. Or if you travel by motor-caravan you could write from that aspect – how easy it is to find places to camp, places of interest en route, problems encountered by travelling this way, and so on. Paul Theroux loves trains and writes about what happens to him and the people he meets while travelling on them. Fascinating.

Zero in on those aspects of a place that appeal to *you*. What are the little details that stick in your mind long after the holiday is over? Perhaps you remember those warm evenings in Florence, when you took things easy after a day of visiting museums and churches. You remember the delicious pleasure in sitting at a sidewalk café doing nothing in particular, or the little bars and restaurants you discovered from wandering around the back streets. 'Evenings in Florence' could be the focus for your article and would give readers a different view than that usually found in guide books and travel articles.

Specialised knowledge

If you are a beginner in the travel-writing field and wondering where to start, think about what you do in your daily life. You probably have a job, a hobby or a skill that could be incorporated into a travel piece, giving you an edge over the predictable kind of travel articles that editors groan over.

If you are interested in photography, the travel-writing world is your oyster. Not only can you double your money by selling pictures with your article (more about this in Chapter 8), you can also come up with original and fascinating ideas based on the photographs you have taken. If you are particularly interested in photographing flowers, for instance, you could write a piece something along the lines of 'Flower-Filled Fiji' or 'The Desert Blooms'. The possibilities are endless.

Perhaps you like to ski and have tried many different resorts. Skiing is rapidly growing in popularity and each autumn the travel sections of newspapers and magazines carry dozens of pieces on all aspects of the sport. If you know a place which is particularly good for beginners, write about it. Tell the reader what they can expect to find; what the après-ski activities are like and which resorts they can visit in the surrounding area.

If you like to cook and are interested in the cuisines of other cultures there are scores of opportunities to combine your culinary knowledge with a travel article. Many publications feature food and travel pieces. It's a very popular topic and most people are interested in this combination. *Taste* magazine has published a number of articles such as 'The Taste of Denmark' or 'The Taste of Tuscany' – pieces which not only conjure up tastes but a vision of the country as well. And you don't have to travel far. An article on

'The Taste of Scotland', for instance, could have just as much appeal.

British people are renowned for their love of walking and there are many magazines which deal with all aspects of this activity. If you enjoy walking or hiking there are plenty of editors just waiting for an interesting article from you. Have you discovered good places to eat and good hotels to stay in while on your walks? If so, share them by writing a piece about them. Something like 'The Six Best B & Bs on the Pennine Way' might sell. Use your imagination. Are there any famous people connected with your favourite walks? Perhaps you could write something like 'Walking with the Brontës' or 'Thomas Hardy Walked Here'. Once you start thinking along these lines you'll find lots of ideas. And it's great fun doing the research – just think of all those lovely walks.

Whatever your hobbies or interests are, try to think of them in terms of travel writing. You'll be surprised at how even the most esoteric hobby can be used in a travel piece.

Angle for the editor's attention

Writers often talk about 'ideas' and 'angles' in the same breath, and the words are usually interchangeable. For me, the word 'angle' suggests a particularly sharp idea, one that has been polished and honed to the point where it is instantly intriguing.

When an editor asks, 'What is the angle?', she is asking you what specific approach you have taken in regard to the subject you have chosen. For example, in one of the books from *The Sophisticated Traveller* series, there is an article by Joseph Heller entitled 'Oslo: Meet Me at the Café.' With all of the city of Oslo at hand, the author chose to write about one very particular spot, the Theatercafeen, which he describes as 'a spacious and bustling eating and drinking haunt that is known throughout the city as the busiest place in town'. After reading this article I longed to go and sit in the Theatercafeen, eat the open sandwiches and cups of tiny local shrimp in Russian dressing that Heller wrote about, and get a taste of Oslo life.

Another writer may have chosen to write a piece about Oslo's café life in general. The result would perhaps have been a fuzzier, less focused article without the pungent appeal of the Theatercafeen. I know that when I visit Oslo I shall make straight for it.

When writers tell everything about their trip they sometimes overload the reader with too much information, much of which they may already know. Try to narrow your focus and aim for a unique point of view. A destination may be old hat to many people, but if it is a first-time visit for you, you will see it with a fresh eye. Write about what it is that delights and surprises you.

The following extract from an article on Turkey by Liam McAuliffe, which appeared in *The Sunday Times*, illustrates how the writer chose to write about a very specific aspect of his experience of Turkey:

It began on April Fool's Day, which seemed appropriate. The whole world and his dog had told me it was a lunatic undertaking. But I was chasing a dream. Seventeen months previous I had travelled the breadth of Turkey en route to the Himalayas.

   In Goreme, Cappadocia, in the middle of the night, I was bewitched by carpets. Not cheap bazaar rugs but the brilliant colour of the *yacibedirs* woven for centuries by the nomads of the Eastern peaks and plains.

He goes on to describe how he travelled to Milas, a

renowned carpet region, and the enjoyment he – and the carpet sellers – got from haggling for hours over glasses of tea.

From this article I learned something about Turkish carpets, something about the nature of haggling – how necessary it is – and tasted a little of the life of the bazaars – more than I might have got from a piece which tried to tell me everything in one fell swoop.

Dear to all editors' hearts are freelances who come up with ideas that are original and specific. Don't try the editor's patience with ideas that have not been thought through clearly and are too wide in their scope. Specific angling makes the difference between a yes and a yawn.

Another profitable aspect of specificity is that you will frequently be able to come up with three or four different ideas from one subject. For example, I had a holiday in South America where I visited Peru and Bolivia. Rather than attempt to write one article about the trip – much too big a subject – I selected some specific aspects of it. I wrote a piece for the *Guardian* on the Peruvian jungle, and two pieces for a magazine in Singapore on Machu Picchu and La Paz.

The angle is what makes an article right for one publication and wrong for another. With good market research you will be able to slant your pieces in the right direction. Many a perfectly good article is rejected because the angle is wrong for the readership. There's not much point in sending a piece on 'Walking in the Cotswolds' to an adventurous travel magazine like *Special Interest Holidays* which publishes pieces about trekking in Nepal, scuba diving, and surviving in the Bush. But it might be just right for the more sedate *Lady*.

Another benefit of having a strong angle is that it will make it easier for you to write the article. The research you do for the piece will be concentrated on this one particular angle, rather than on the subject as a whole.

Beware the demon cliché

As the golden sun sinks in the west, take another look at your travel article. It may contain writing such as the following opening paragraph for a piece on Hawaii:

> As the graceful white liner moved softly over the water towards Hawaii strains of hula music drifted from the shore, and as we berthed at Honolulu we were delighted to see a welcoming group of happy Polynesian faces raised to greet us. They wore fragrant leis around their necks and strummed their guitars to the sinuous movements of a pretty hula dancer whose black hair hung to her waist.

And on it goes in a similar vein. Yawn. This was written by a beginner – myself. It was a long time ago and of course it was rejected.

Beginners tend to write in a clichéd manner. Many words that jump instantly to mind are clichés because they are overused and tired. Compare the above opening paragraph with that of a piece on Corsica written by Julia Butt and published in *The Best of Sunday Times Travel*.

> Napoleon greeted us when we arrived in the palm-fringed port of Ajaccio and disembarked on to the jetty. Corsica's capital exhibits boulevards, bars and boats in honour of its most famous son. The white-glossed vessels glide out slowly with their cargoes of rich French and Italian mariners, perhaps south to Sardinia or Sicily

before venturing upon Poseidon's homeland in the depths of the Aegean.

Note the difference.

To write well you must try to avoid clichés. Clichéd writing indicates a lack of care about the words the writer has chosen. The English language is one of the richest in the world and if you are to be a writer, a wordsmith, you must try to avoid writing that is commonplace and predictable.

Use the dictionary or a thesaurus to find other meanings for words. Play around with visual images so that you don't write as I did in my Hawaii piece. To begin with the liner steaming into harbour is too obvious. Instead of spelling it out I could perhaps have introduced the piece by talking about the moment when, at sea, I first smelled land, and the image of Hawaii it conjured up.

As well as being words which are overused, clichés become clichés because they are usually accurate and convenient to use. High mountains *are* awe-inspiring. Beaches *are* golden. The Mediterranean *is* azure blue. So what? The reader knows that. It has all been said before, many times. What he or she wants to read about is the writer's own unique way of making a point. Readers don't respect cliché-users. If the writer has not taken the trouble to express himself in a manner that is fresh, with words carefully chosen, then the reader gets the impression that he is lazy. And so he is. Tired wording reflects tired thinking.

Some writers needlessly use clichéd foreign phrases such as *terra firma* or *la dolce vita*. Don't do it. It looks pretentious.

If it was raining cats and dogs when you were in Torquay, don't tell the reader that. Avoid clichés like the plague. And there's another cliché!

Show, don't tell

Many novice travel writers fail to sell their articles because they tell too much and show too little. In other words, they use too many adjectives and not enough word pictures. It's no good saying something like 'We drove up the mountain and there was a lovely view from the summit.' The reader wants to know how it looked, smelled and tasted. How did the breeze feel against your skin? Was there perfume in the air? Was the mountain bathed in sunlight? How did it all affect you? Don't say 'there was an unpleasant smell'. Describe the smell. Did it remind you of rotten fruit or burnt rubber? A good travel article is essentially a picture painted with words, so try to paint a picture with your words that enables the reader to experience what you experienced.

'Show, don't tell' means getting rid of all those words which really don't tell the reader anything very much about the place. After all, what does the word 'beautiful' mean? It could mean something different for everyone. If you talk about a 'beautiful scene', what is conjured up in the mind of the reader may be something entirely different to what was actually there. And if you use too many adjectives like this you may never get the opportunity to have readers. When an editor says 'Show, don't tell', she is telling you to get rid of all those words which don't contribute to the visual image you are trying to give and replace them with words that count.

An example of showing is the following paragraph, taken from an article in *World Magazine* on hill-walking, written by Nick Crane.

Round the edge of Mirror Lake lay the dried white trunks of trees, bleached like the bones of old whales. A fish flipped, silver in the sun, and plopped back into the black water, little ripples worrying the image of the mountain that lay on its surface with the clarity of a photograph. The only sound came from the trees behind us: a wistful sigh as the warming morning air rose from the dusty pan of Owens Valley far below to breathe its heat on the high cold granite.

What a picture that paints! How flat and uninteresting it would have been if he had merely described the lake as 'calm', or the morning air as 'hot'.

In Chapter 2 I emphasised the importance of keeping a journal. If you vividly and sensitively record your reactions to your surroundings, noting things like smells, colours, textures and so on, you will have a good source to draw upon when you write your article.

Travel writing is like being in the entertainment business – you have to keep the audience interested. You can do this by painting a vivid word picture that will keep them glued to their seats until the end.

Rewriting – cut, cut, cut

You've written your article, said all you have to say, and now you sit back to read it over. Whatever you do, don't even think of sending it off to an editor. When you reread your manuscript as soon as it is finished it is almost impossible to spot imperfections – and I can guarantee there will be some. At this point you are much too close to your creation to be objective, and the thought of cutting out phrases and sentences that you've slaved over can be very painful. What you should do at this moment is put the manuscript in a drawer, go and make a cup of tea, visit a friend, or do anything that will take your mind off it for a while. Ideally, don't peek at it again for at least three days.

Instead, try to begin a new writing project immediately. When you do take your first piece out of the drawer you will be able to edit your work with a clearer, more objective editorial eye.

My dictionary says the word 'edit' means 'prepare for publication', and to professional writers this means rewriting and more rewriting. A first draft is almost always overwritten – rewriting gives you the opportunity to clean up carelessly repeated words and clumsy sentences, to smarten up dull paragraphs, smooth out awkward transitions, and get rid of clichés.

Almost all writing is improved by cutting and rewriting. Look at the following example.

First draft:

> Our guide was an extremely capable man and he also had the ability to make us have confidence. We learned to man the canoes, get the campfire going, and put up the tents before we'd even got over our jet lag. (41 words)

Second draft:

> Our guide was very capable and convinced us we were too. We learned to deal with canoes and campsites before we'd even got over jet lag. (26 words)

Reading your piece out loud can be very useful in helping you spot flaws. Sentences that seem fine on the page sometimes sound as if they are going on for ever, and puns and clichés practically leap from the page.

The more times you go over your article the more words you will discover you can cut out. Spareness and economy in writing makes it lively and more readable.

Novice writers often feel they have to tell everything. They feel the reader won't understand what they are saying unless they spell everything out. All this kind of writing does, in fact, is slow the piece down and make it soggy and heavy with extra words and phrases.

Do try to be very strict with yourself when you are editing your work. Be merciless in your cutting and get rid of every unnecessary word, fact, phrase or sentence. Economy of style should be your goal. Remember, as Voltaire said, 'The secret of being boring is to tell everything.'

Transitions – a smooth journey

Now you have your article cleaned up, cut down to size, and almost ready to go. Before you send it off, take one last look at it. Is it as wrinkle-free as it can possible be? One way to ensure this is to check your transitions.

A transition is like a sign that points the reader in the direction you want him to go and words and phrases like 'therefore', 'however', 'nevertheless', 'on the contrary', 'as a result' can make the passage from one paragraph to another smooth and effortless. For example, if you are writing a piece on travelling around a particular area by car and on foot, you might end a paragraph with something like, 'That's the best reason for doing this stretch by car', and begin the next paragraph with 'On the other hand [the transition], your feet can take you places the car cannot reach.'

Some transitions, like those mentioned above for instance, are overworked. Good transitions can make your writing more stylish and coherent, so try to find less obvious ways to give your reader a smooth passage. There are many devices you can use, such as comparing and contrasting. For instance, your paragraph may end with 'At the end of the long hike the guide produced a flask of delicious hot coffee which we drank thirstily and gratefully.' The following paragraph could start: 'The cup of tea we got the following morning was not so well received. Lukewarm and colourless, it was not a good start to the day.'

Another useful transitional device is time: 'later that day', 'next morning', 'the following day'. You can also repeat the last word or sentence of the previous paragraph, for instance if a paragraph ends with 'the light of the setting sun was brilliant', you could start the next paragraph with 'Brilliant was not how I felt the following morning as the boat heaved against the huge waves.' Or, 'We thought we would spend some time in the village at the foot of the mountain looking for souvenirs.' Next paragraph begins: 'Souvenir-hunting disappeared from our minds as we came to the end of the village and saw the long climb ahead of us.'

In *The Old Patagonian Express*, Paul Theroux writes:

> At a side chapel was the Virgin of Chiquiniquira, a black madonna with an ebony face. Black Guatemalans . . . had prostrated themselves before the nigrescent Virgin who, 'loaded down with sumptuous toys,' remarks Morelet, 'receives exclusively the homage of the faithful of the African race.'
>
> Travellers less sympathetic than Morelet – one supposes them to be unyielding Protestants – have seen Guatemalan Catholicism as barbarous.

Note the smooth transition the writer has achieved by repeating the name 'Morelet'.

As you rewrite, look for more subtle ways to make smooth transitions. Good transitions have been described as helping the reader catch your train of thought without getting derailed. The less bumpy you can make the ride, the better.

5

MARKETING (1) – MARKET RESEARCH

One of the hardest lessons a freelance writer must learn is to direct an article to a specific audience. The periodical market is huge; over 7,000 are published each year. Add to this national and local newspapers and it's not surprising that beginners recoil in confusion.

How to start

It has often been said that while amateurs talk about writing, professionals talk about marketing. It's true, they do. A person who is trying to make a living at writing cannot afford to waste time and money sending out articles to publications in the hope that they might just be lucky and hit the jackpot. There are too many variables involved; some magazines never take pieces on exotic travel locations because their readership is mostly composed of people who could not afford such trips. Others specialise in the kind of far-out travel that people like to read about but not necessarily undertake. I mean, how many of us really want to follow in the footsteps of the Yeti? Yet such articles are perfect for the armchair traveller.

If you are really serious about selling your work you must

do as the professionals do and study the market. This is not as overwhelming as it seems. I suggest you select three or four publications, preferably different in style and readership. Spend some time browsing through magazines in your local newsagent and pick out those that have travel sections; you'll be surprised at how many do. Choose one of the many weekly women's magazines such as *Best, Bella*, or the *Lady*. Remember that the weeklies are published four times as often as the monthlies, so you have more opportunities with them.

If you take a daily newspaper, check out its weekly travel section and add it to your market list. The same applies to the weekend newspapers which, with the supplements, are taking more travel articles than ever before.

Choose a monthly magazine that appeals to your own taste. Perhaps you are fond of good food and wine and could write an appetising travel piece built around your trip to Provence, for example. In this case a magazine such as *Taste* might be worth adding to your list.

There are a number of magazines which specialise purely in travel writing – select one of these for your research.

As well as checking out the newsagents for possible markets, you should beg or borrow magazines from friends or ask your hairdresser, dentist or doctor to let you have their cast-offs. The more magazines you read, the more you will become aware of who takes travel pieces and what they are looking for. It's also a great way to get new ideas.

Buy copies of your chosen publications each week or month until you have five or six copies of each. Regard this expenditure as an investment. The glossiest of magazines rarely costs more than £2.00 – less than you pay for an evening at the cinema.

Every writer should own a copy of either the *Writers' & Artists' Yearbook* or *The Writer's Handbook* (I have both and find each equally useful). Both of these publications are annuals and contain detailed guides to markets as well as helpful information on contracts, copyright, etc. Suppose you have chosen the magazine *Traveller* as one of your target markets. This is what the 1991 edition of each handbook has to say:

Writers' & Artists' Yearbook:
Traveller (1970), Wexas Ltd, 45 Brompton Road, London, SW3 1DE, tel 071–581–4130, telegraphic address Wexas London SW3, telex 297155 Wexas G, fax 071–589–8418. £30.67 p.a. 3 p.a. Features on independent travel of all kinds but specialising in long-haul and off-beat destinations with first-class photographs. Articles giving useful tips on particular aspects of travel, country and city reports providing insight and factual information of use to other travellers. Articles not strictly on travel but of related interest also welcomed. Length: 1,000 to 2,000 words. Payment: rates and leaflet giving full details of requirements available, s.a.e. required.

The Writer's Handbook
Traveller. 45 Brompton Road, London SW3 1DE. Tel. 071–581–4130. Fax 071–589–8418 Telex. 297155 WEXAS G.
Owner Dr I. M. Wilson, Wexas.
Editor Sacra Gorman
Circulation 33,000
Founded 1970. Three issues yearly. Unsolicited mss welcome, but a preliminary letter is preferred.
Features Five colour features per issue – authors should supply pictures. Contributors' guidelines available with s.a.e., but all articles should be off-beat, independent, and travel-based. Maximum 2,000 words. Payment £50 per 1000 words.

From the above you will probably see why I like to have both copies. *The Writers' & Artists' Yearbook* gives some information that *The Writer's Handbook* does not, and vice versa.

Don't be put off by the large number of magazines listed in the writers' handbooks. The time will come when you will be targeting quite a few of them, but for the time being it is best to concentrate on the publications you have chosen. If you concentrate your thoughts and energy on these you are much more likely to come up with something that is tailored to their requirements and has a good chance of being accepted.

Who are you writing for?

Now that you have your starter set of target markets the first thing to do is to get to know your prospective readers, and a good way to do this is to check the ads, especially if you have chosen publications that you are unfamiliar with.

Advertising agencies have to come up with ads that will evoke response from the reader; that will encourage him or her to buy the product they have so cleverly packaged. Take advantage of their expertise – they cannot afford to misjudge their target readers. Advertising costs hundreds of pounds per page and this revenue, not the cover charge which hardly provides for basic expenses like running the office and paying freelance writers, is what keeps the magazine going.

The ads can tell you more about the readership than anything else. Are they for the latest thing in sportswear and equipment, or for kitchens and babies' nappies? Are there pages of expensive cars, whisky and perfume, or are they full of shopping catalogues, DIY kits, and tea bags? You must know who you are writing for.

The ads will give you lots of clues and will indicate the reader's income bracket, interests and hobbies, what kind of holiday he/she likes, and much more. Once you have formed a firm opinion of the reader, this is the person to keep in mind when writing for the publication. With careful market research article writers get to know their potential readers very well. Knowing your target audience can make all the difference between acceptance and rejection. Looking at the merchandise advertised will give you a good idea of your reader's lifestyle and what he considers worth spending his money on, but you also need to have an idea of his preoccupations. The contents of the magazine will tell you what his interests and hobbies are – if he is sports-minded you could write about tennis, skiing or golfing resorts. What are her concerns and biases? If she is interested in environmental issues there may be scope for pieces on places you have visited which are involved in conservation schemes or perhaps a resort which has made extensive efforts to keep its beaches pollution-free. What kind of food does he/she like? Check the cookery pages – do they write about barbecues, packed lunches or *haute cuisine?* Check the letters page, the travel page. Ask yourself what the articles are about. Make notes, and as you do you will gradually come up with a clear picture of your prospective reader. Good travel writing should always be directed to a specific reader and if you do your homework well a clear picture of this reader will emerge. Keep this picture in mind when writing your article and try not to stray from it.

Suppose you have decided to target the *Lady*, which is a good market for beginners, you might come up with an analysis of a *Lady* reader something along the following lines:

Reader Profile: The ads for tweedy skirts, cord jackets, hand-crafted furniture, animal sanctuaries and numer-

ous charities indicate a middle-class readership, probably mostly country dwellers. The situations vacant col-
umns are full of requests for nannies and housekeepers,
which indicates a certain amount of affluence. Travel
articles are along the lines of 'Sidmouth – A Floral
Town for Fisherman', 'An Update on Spain's Sun
Coast', or 'All Change at Docklands'. Probably a fairly
conservative type of readership and one that is unlikely
to be interested in way-out travel pieces, or destinations
where you have to 'rough it'. Other *Lady* features cover
historical profiles, gardening, cookery and nostalgia,
indicating that the typical reader is in the age group
from about 35 upwards.

From the above, you would hardly be likely to send the
Lady an article on hitch-hiking across Australia, but they
might be interested in something on your stay in a French
château.
Go through your three or four chosen target markets
carefully and draw up a reader profile for each one. It's
worth spending a bit of time on this as it will pay off in the
long run. Put the reader profiles aside for the moment. They
are important pieces of market research and will be included
in the overall market analysis.

How to analyse a magazine

It is important to learn how to develop an analytical
approach toward your prospective markets. Later, when
you are accustomed to looking at publications with a critical
(marketing) eye, you will be able to sum up the readership,
editorial requirements and general tone without too much
trouble. Now it all probably seems confusing, but if you put

in the effort to learn how to analyse magazines correctly in the beginning it will pay off later in terms of sales.

Having looked carefully at your target publication and come up with a reader profile as well as an idea of what the magazine is about in general, you should now begin to think more specifically about travel writing. Go through each publication slowly and carefully and make up a target information sheet by writing down every bit of information that will be of use to you. Read each travel article carefully and make notes as you go. Note the style. Is the language formal or informal? Do they use anecdotes and quotes? Are the articles written in first person or third? Note the name of the travel editor – there is a staff list (called the masthead) printed somewhere in most magazines, or you can telephone and get this information from the switchboard operator; this applies to newspapers too.

If the same byline (author's name) appears week after week it usually means that those pieces are written by a staff writer and there will not be much opportunity for freelance work. If you have had to buy three or four copies of the publication to find this out don't regard it as a waste of time and money; the more reading you do the more you become aware of what is being written and, again, it can act as a trigger for new ideas. Look for a new target market to replace this one.

Count the words in two or three articles from each publication to find the average length and add this to your information sheet. There's no point in sending a 1,500-word piece to a publication that never takes anything over 800 words. Do as much as you can to save yourself, and the editor, time.

Suppose you have decided to target *Cosmopolitan*. This is a magazine aimed at young women of about 25, usually single, whose main interests – as you will see when you do your market research on the articles – are work and love.

What is of interest to you as a travel writer is that they carry a travel piece each month and that it comes from a freelance. You'll discover this from reading a few issues and noticing that the bylines are different each time.

From checking the ads and the general contents you have made up a reader profile and you should now have a clear picture of the *Cosmopolitan* reader. Keep this person in mind when you have completed your market analysis and are deciding on an approach.

To make up Target Information Sheets, start with basic information from your writer's handbook. This saves you looking up the magazine every time you want the address, telephone number, etc.

Cut out the travel articles from four or five issues of your target publications, date them, and clip them to your target information sheet. This gives you an idea of the kind of piece the editor is looking for and also saves you having to thumb through a pile of magazines every time you want to check out what they have already published.

Some publications produce guidelines which they will send to you if you write (with s.a.e.). These are invaluable as they tell you exactly what the editor requires. Add them to your target information file. By now you should have gathered enough information on your target markets to know what they are looking for. All you have to do now is write.

A typical Target Information Sheet might look like this:

Cosmopolitan

Writers' and Artists' Yearbook

Cosmopolitan (1972), Marcelle D'Argy Smith, National Magazine House, 72 Broadwick Street, London, W1V 2BP. Tel 071–439–5000, fax 071–437–6886. £1.00. M. Short stories, articles. Commissioned material only. Payment by arrangement.

The Writers' Handbook

Cosmopolitan Tel. 071–439–7144 (Phone No. different from W & A Yearbook?) Fax 071–437–6886.
Owner National Magazine Co. Ltd.
Editor Marcelle D'Argy Smith
Circulation 396,000
Popular mix of articles, emotional advice and strong fiction designed to appeal to the early-twenties modern-minded female. Known to have a policy of not considering unsolicited mss, but does nevertheless sometimes look at those it receives as it is always on the lookout for new writers. 'The thing to do is to ring the features desk with an idea; if they are interested they will ask to see something.'

Market Analysis

Advertisements. Mostly for cosmetics, sun protection creams, fashion, perfume, medium-priced cars, diet products. Has the occasional ad for furniture, washing machines, bathrooms.
General Articles. Thundering Thatcher. The Decline and Fall of London. Love is better on a beach. Holloway – the inside story. What I learned from my parents' marriage. Freelance finance. Watersports (wind-surfing, water-skiing). What men talk about when they talk about women. Are unit trusts worth a try?
Travel Articles. Insider's Paris. Locomotion USA (travelling across America by train). Have a weekend fling in France. Electrifying New York. I'll take St Lucia. The Ease and Charm of Amsterdam.

Style of writing. The travel articles are destination pieces with plenty of information on how to get there and how much it costs. Mostly written in the first person. Not many anecdotes or sidelines. Practical information on shopping (when applicable). Simple, straightforward writing. Not chatty but not bland either. Not difficult to tackle. Unusual angles or points of view.

Number of words. Between 1,000 and 1,500.

Reader Profile. Young, single woman, early twenties. Interested in looking good and keeping healthy. From the quality of merchandise advertised she probably has a fairly good job and is interested in a career – i.e. the articles on finance, unit trusts, etc. Probably not a professional but fairly intelligent and interested in current affairs as well as in men – how to meet them, what they think, etc. Travel pieces indicate an adventurous spirit – a person who doesn't mind a challenge. Can't afford top luxury but able to afford medium-priced holidays.

How to organise an efficient marketing system

You have chosen your target markets, you have analysed them, you know the readership, you are ready to go. Now what?

Let's look at four publications from those mentioned so far in this book. Perhaps the *Lady* and *Bella* (both weeklies but quite different in style and content), the *Guardian* and the *Traveller*. This represents a good variety; two weekly women's magazines, one newspaper, and one travel magazine.

Make up a target information sheet for each one – see the example for *Cosmopolitan* – and file in a loose-leaf binder. (I have purposely *not* given one of the above men-

tioned magazines as an example. You must do your own –
it will be far more valuable to you than anything I produce.)

Now you have four separate markets ready to tackle.
Which one should you try first?

Suppose you want to write a piece about a cycling holiday
in Holland. Look at the subject. You can probably rule out
the *Lady* as you will note from the readership analysis (see
mine on page 66–7) that they are somewhat conservative
and probably not interested in anything that smacks of
'roughing it'. Discount the *Lady* for this piece.

What about the *Guardian*? It's a possibility. As you will
have noticed, the *Guardian* travel pages are very eclectic,
and much depends on the angle you have chosen. Rather
than a straightforward account, the editor might be interested in difficulties encountered en route, or how easy it is
to get off the beaten track when travelling by bicycle. Sift
through your material and choose an appropriate approach.

Bella is written for women who are probably at home
with children. For obvious reasons they are unlikely at this
point to be taking a cycling holiday – the hazards involved
with small children being just one. But, depending on the
angle, it might work.

That leaves the *Traveller*. From the information on your
target information sheet, taken from the writers' yearbooks,
you will see they want features on independent travel of all
kinds but specialising in off-beat destinations with first-class
photographs. If your cycling holiday has taken you to off-
beat places this might very well be the market to try for,
but unless you have good photographs it may be difficult to
sell your article.

From the above, it seems that from our four target markets the *Guardian* and the *Traveller* are the most likely
prospects to tackle first with your cycling holiday piece.
Decide which one to begin with and whether or not to query
the editor first (see Chapter 7). Now get on with writing it.

In the beginning it is essential to keep as many articles in circulation as possible. When you have written your first piece and sent it out to one of your target markets, don't wait around biting your fingernails until you get a reply. Tackle another target and get another article into the post as soon as possible. If you have three or four pieces out you won't suffer from the sting of rejection quite so much as you would if your one and only article flops through the letterbox in the self-addressed envelope you sent to the editor. There will always be hope that the others will be accepted.

In the early stages of learning about marketing you often have to send out your work to a number of publications in order to hit the right one. Of course you will have to rewrite the pieces according to the individual readerships and requirements, and you may have to rewrite from an entirely different angle. This will become easier with time. You already have all the information, it's just a matter of presenting it in a different way.

Even when you have carefully studied the magazine or newspaper before sending out your article, there are many reasons why the editor might reject it. One of the most common is that they have something similar in the works for an upcoming issue – a good reason why you should query first. If an editor writes and tells you this, be encouraged. If your piece was completely unsuitable you would usually get no more than a standard rejection slip. So send the editor something else immediately.

As you write more articles you will discover how important it is to keep careful track of everything: which publications you have contacted, who you are waiting to hear from, and so on.

Following is a simple, efficient system for keeping track of your work. Remember that each submission has to be written specifically for the market you are submitting to.

ARTICLE – FREEWHEELING AROUND HOLLAND
(Re cycling holiday) – 1,000 words.

Sent to:	Date sent	Date replied	Yes or No	Comments
Traveller	7 April 90	26 May 90	No	Already covered, but they liked it. Suggested sending more.
Bella	6 June 90	1 July 90	No	No particular comments. Form rejection slip.
The Guardian	15 August 90	28 August (phoned)	Yes	Would like photos.

....

Query letter to:
Travel & 1 Aug 90
Leisure
(USA)*

....

Sold to:		Amount paid	Date Published
The Guardian		£	

FIGURE 5.1. Typical Record of Submissions sheet

*See Chapter 9 re overseas markets.

How to expand your market horizons

Depending upon where you live, it might not always be easy to buy a large selection of travel-related magazines at your local newsagents. One way to build up your stock of potential markets is to go through your marketing handbook(s), make a note of all publications you are interested in, and write to them asking if you can purchase three or four back copies.

Willings Press Guide, published annually, alone lists around 8,000 periodicals. On top of this figure are daily newspapers. It also lists newspapers, periodicals and annuals in Europe, the Americas, Australasia, the Far East, and the Middle East. Your local library will probably have a copy. Spend some time browsing through its pages; you'll find many potential travel markets.

There are a number of writers' magazines which contain very helpful market lists. *Freelance Market News*, for instance, is concerned solely with markets. Published monthly, it lists UK and overseas markets and gives information on what their requirements are, how much they pay, whether they prefer to receive queries or complete manuscripts.

Other useful publications which include marketing information are *Writers News* and *Writers' Monthly*. The latter has a competition each month, which sometimes is for a travel article. Get into the habit of looking through *every* magazine you come across to see if it has a travel section – many unlikely looking ones do and a lot of them are free. For example, Sealink British Ferries publish *Connections*. In one issue they had articles on Amsterdam's café society, motoring abroad, and exploring Burgundy and Bordeaux. British Rail's magazine *Intercity* is another freebie which contains travel features on subjects such as life in the Cheviots. Avis produces *Personally Yours*, with pieces like 'Coasting Along – The Best of British Resorts', and a look at the once industrious mill towns of Yorkshire in 'Mill Towns Revisited'.

Free magazines can be found on the streets of most of Britain's major cities. In London there is *Ms London, TNT* and *Nine to Five*, to name just a few. They take a variety of articles, including travel.

If you are interested in exploring the wide world of free publications you should contact the Association of Free Newspapers (AFN) and the Association of Free Magazines and Periodicals (AFMP) at Ladybellegate House, Longsmith Street, Gloucester GL1 2HT. Ask for the current issues of *Free Magazine Review* and *AFN News*.

Trade publications are another unexpected source for travel writing. Ask your friends and relatives if there is a specialist magazine published for their profession or business. Many include travel articles and you'd have a real chance of a sale if you could tie in your piece with their own particular line of interest. For example, if you have had an unfortunate (or even fortunate) experience with a dentist while travelling in the Australian outback you might be able to interest one of the dental publications.

Retirement magazines are another good market. Many people who take early retirement have the time, money and energy to travel and they provide an ever-widening audience for the travel writer. If you can't find any in your local newsagents, look them up in your writers' market book and write for a sample copy. *Choice* and *Yours* are two that you might want to investigate.

There are dozens of hobby magazines on the newsagent's shelves and whereas these may not seem obvious markets for travel articles there's always the possibility that your own hobbies could be combined with a travel piece and sold to them. For instance, if you are a keen sailor you might write something about how you and your boat survived a storm off the coast of Portugal, and perhaps go on to describe the attractions of the pretty little harbour town where you moored. Or, if you like gardening the possibilities are endless; there are beautiful gardens in almost every country you are likely to visit. Why not write about them? *Willings Press Guide* lists over a dozen gardening publications and three times as many for yachting and boating.

There is even a magazine for beermat collectors, called *Beermat Magazine*. If you have some unusual beermats which you collected in strange places you have the ingredients for an interesting article.

As I mentioned earlier, 'Write about what you know' is the advice given in most books on article writing. If you can combine your particular knowledge with travel writing you will increase your potential markets enormously.

Once you have begun to 'think markets' you will find possibilities cropping up all over the place. By keeping your eyes open for new target markets and gradually adding them to your file you'll end up with a carefully chosen comprehensive list that will allow you to keep your work in circulation. But a word of warning for the beginner – don't take on too much too soon. Yes, get together as many potential markets as you can but remember to choose no more than four or five for your initial approach. Marketing is hard work. It takes time, and trying to deal with the requirements of too many publications at the same time can be very confusing.

6

MARKETING (2) – STRUCTURE AND STYLE

Style distinguishes a writer's work, but what is it? Ask six different people for their definition of style and you will get six different answers. It is almost impossible to define.

What is style?

All that can be said with any certainty is that style is the manner in which a writer expresses his or her individuality. There are no rules like those of grammar, which, if faithfully followed, will give you an individual style. Your style will evolve out of the words you choose and the manner in which they are arranged. Like music, where a particular arrangement of notes can produce a beautiful melody, the way a writer arranges words can produce a fine style. Take the same notes, arrange them in a different way, and the result may be discord. Similarly, rearrange the words of a fine sentence or passage and style will vanish. For example, Robert Louis Stevenson wrote: 'To travel hopefully is a better thing than to arrive.' This is a simple sentence, composed of ten easy words, yet it is still often quoted more

than a century after it was written. Why is this? The answer
is that it has style. Compare the following variations

- – to be hopeful when you travel is better than arriving.
- – Arriving is not as good as travelling hopefully.
- – To travel hopefully makes arriving better.

I doubt Stevenson's words would have survived if he had
written them in any of these forms. But why not? There is
nothing wrong with them, yet they are wooden and forget-
table.

In his book *On Writing and the Novel* Paul Scott says: 'I
was once asked by someone to say what style was and how
it could be acquired. I said that style was the individual tone
of voice, and could not be taught. A singer can be trained
to do things like breathe correctly and phrase felicitously.
He can be taught how to get the best out of his voice, but
the voice itself is what he begins and ends with. So it is with
the writer.'

How then does the new writer find the key to this mystery
that style is? Like singers, writers must develop their own
voice – it should show in their work – but how do they do
it?

It is important in the beginning not to worry too much
about style. As you become more confident in your own
observations and your ability to put them down on paper,
and as you learn to write freely and openly, your own style
will gradually emerge. Become aware of style by reading
with an analytical eye those authors whom you admire. Ask
yourself what it is about their writing that you like. Do they
use short, terse sentences that give their writing an intense
quality? If you like to write travel articles about adventurous, off-beat places, you may find a tight style captures the
excitement and tension you are trying to convey. Or perhaps
your favourite travel writers use a more lyrical, descriptive

style, better suited to a more relaxed, languorous approach to travelling.

The use of language begins with imitation. We learned to talk by imitating our parents, so don't be afraid to learn about style by imitating those travel writers you admire. In time you will learn to write naturally, in your own way.

Here are a few hints that may help you find your own style:

– Try to write naturally. Use words that come readily to mind. Have the confidence to describe places, people, smells, colours and sounds in words of your own that express what *you* feel.

– Plan ahead. Have an idea of what you are going to write about. This does not mean you have to have a blueprint of your trip from which you cannot deviate. What a plan will do for you is leave you free to take in your surroundings with all your senses, and make notes in your journal, without being distracted by deciding where you should go next, what you should look at, etc.

– Write clearly. Tempting as it may be when you are writing about exotic, foreign places, do try to resist using foreign words or phrases. Clarity is what you should strive for. Don't be afraid to use plain English – eventually your own voice will come through.

The seventeenth-century French writer and philosopher, Pascal, said: 'When one finds a natural style, one is amazed and delighted, for where one expected to see an author, one discovers a man.'

Structure of the article

A good travel article has a beginning, a middle, and an end. The beginning is what entices the reader – and the editor –

to read on; the middle provides facts, colourful descriptions and useful information, and the end ties everything together in a satisfactory manner.

Beginnings

The first paragraph must convince the reader that your article is worth reading. Sometimes called the lead or the hook, the opening is crucial. It should pull the reader in and involve him or her in what you have to say. Because the opening is so important, finding one that has impact and does all it is supposed to do can be quite difficult. Many beginning travel writers find this intimidating. When you have so much to say about a place, where do you begin? If you are having difficulty there are various types of openings that you can use to get you going.

The descriptive opening sets the scene; it presents a vivid visual image that draws the reader in. She can see the landscape in her mind's eye, feel the heat and smell the earth. She wants to know more.

Writing about British Guiana in *The Middle Passage*, V. S. Naipaul opens with the following paragraph:

From the air Trinidad's Atlantic coast was outlined as on the map, the waves steadily rolling lace-patterned foam towards the shore, green edged with yellow. The waves began far out and rolled in evenly. On the bright blue water cloud shadows were like submerged rocks or like dissolving drops of ink. Soon blue water turned to brown, its progressively darker shades neatly contoured and sometimes marked off in white. Then the South American continent: a grey-green tufted carpet, worn brown in patches, with rivers like cracks in drying mud. For minute after minute we moved rapidly over

81

the unchanging, unwelcoming land, a small corner of a vast continent, trees grew and collapsed on muddy shores.

Note the phrases and adjectives he has used: *steadily-rolling lace-patterned foam, a grey-green tufted carpet, rivers like cracks in drying mud.* How observant and imaginative he is! To capture such scenes with freshness and vitality it is essential that you make good use of your travel notebook. Don't worry and waste time in trying to find particularly elegant or picturesque words. Jot down your first impressions and use them in descriptive openings. The descriptive opening is like the beginning of a well-planned novel; it draws the reader in with a promise of fascinating things to come.

The comparison beginning arouses the reader's curiosity and builds up tension. He wants to read on, to find out what comes next. You can compare times past and present, such as the following opening paragraph of an article I wrote about London theatres:

Attitudes to theatre have changed quite a bit since the days of Queen Elizabeth I, when strolling players made their living on the streets and were often looked upon as vagabonds. In London today there are more than 50 theatres within two square miles and some of the world's greatest actors tread their boards.

Or, you can compare different modes of travelling, as in the following from an article by Betty Cooper, 'A Second Shufti at Jordan', from *The Best of Sunday Times Travel*:

The Queen beat me to it – she got to Petra first! But I doubt if she had as much fun. There she was, a horse-loving woman, bumping through the Siq in a Land

Rover, wearing a skirt and hat. Whereas touristy me – town-bred and with no more knowledge of nags than a few donkey-rides sixty years ago – I rode high and proud on Suzy, a two-year-old Arab who was full of wind and nervous at moving so slowly.

The 'You' beginning is frequently used by travel writers. This technique offers straightforward advice and guidance, as in the following example:

If you want a holiday where your pound buys three times as much as it does at home, where the sun shines ten months of the year, where the beaches are clean and uncrowded and mangoes fall from the trees, make for marvellous Mexico.

There are many other ways to begin your article. Analyse travel features in newspapers and magazines. Notice how they open. See how they complement the rest of the article. Choose the kind of beginning that suits what you have to say and how you want to say it.

Middles

The middle section of your travel article is where you deliver to the reader all that you have promised in your opening paragraph. Here you will develop your point of view in a logical manner; you will give the reader facts, figures and statistics, tell him why he should go, what he can do, what it will cost, how he can get there, and anything else that will back up your argument that this is a worthwhile place to visit.

Use smooth transitions to guide your reader through this middle section. If you want to compare different modes of transport or contrast one beach with another, good transitions will give cohesion to your writing and link up all the information you wish to give into a complete story. See the section on transitions in Chapter 4.

Look again at how V. S. Naipaul opened his article on British Guiana and then see how he enters into the main body of the piece.

> One can learn much about British Guiana from the air: its size, its emptiness, the isolation of its communities. Six hundred thousand people live in a country the size of Britain, and when you fly over the populated eastern coastal strip you see why there is so much unrest in a country, which from its bigness, should be a country of opportunity. The land here is fertile.

He continues in this manner to tell us about the sugarcane fields, to describe the capital, Georgetown, and the Christmas celebrations held there – in short, all we need to know in order to 'see' what British Guiana is like.

If you compare this paragraph with the opening paragraph you will see how important it is to have a strong, enticing lead for your article. Had V. S. Naipaul started with the above opening it would not draw the reader into the story in quite the same way. We are enticed by the colourful descriptions and curious about what is to come as we move 'rapidly over the unchanging unwelcoming land . . .' And having attracted our interest he goes on with the meat of the article.

Endings

Having carefully developed the middle section of your travel article, you should now lead the reader to a satisfactory conclusion. Don't try to end by summarising all that has gone before. The reader knows about that – you do not need to tell him again.

The endings of articles are as important as beginnings. Both serve to tell the reader what the point is. The ending should grow out of the story itself and tie all loose ends neatly together. If you can tie the ending in with the beginning it gives your article a nice 'rounded-off' feeling. For example, you could begin with a question like 'Have you ever wondered why so many people go to Corfu in the summer when it's overcrowded, overheated and overwhelming?' Then, after telling the reader all the good things about Corfu and why so many people go there, you could end with another question such as: 'Ever wondered why so many people go to Corfu? Now you know.'

Or, if you have set the scene with a descriptive opening paragraph, i.e.

As we landed in La Paz the plane seemed to skim the snow from the sparkling mountain tops. This is the highest city in the world, and when the brilliant sunlight rests on peaks up to 21,000 feet high, bathing them in gold, it is a sight not easily forgotten.

The ending might be as follows:

La Paz lay beneath us as we once more flew over the snow-tipped mountains. As the setting sun bathed the slopes in soft bronze light we took with us memories of Bolivia's lush semi-tropical valleys, ancient Inca cities, and above all the charm and hospitality of her people.

Many beginnings do not lend themselves to being tied to endings. If you have trouble in linking up the beginning of your article with the end, don't worry about it. There are many ways to end which are just as effective. Try to make your ending as interesting as possible and avoid petering out or ending too abruptly. Having led your reader through your travel article with a strong opening and an informative, interesting middle, you don't want him to be left feeling dissatisfied or let down by an ending which does not finish off your piece smoothly.

Titles

Good titles catch the reader's eye; like newspaper headlines they are attention-grabbers and they are used on the covers of magazines to lure the browser into buying.

Some travel writers begin an article only when they have a wonderful title to spur them on. They come up with a title which suggests a topic and go on from there. But don't worry if you have difficulty in finding a strong title for your travel article and don't let it prevent you from getting on with the job of writing. You can start with a provisional title which suggests what your story is about, and change it later when you are more inspired. Start with a simple label, such as 'Fabulous Finland' or 'Paris in Winter' and when you have finished writing your article you may be able to come up with something better.

If you have difficulty in finding a good title perhaps you have not thought carefully enough about what you are going to say in your article. If this is the case you should wait until you have completed your piece, read it through carefully for a sharp, interesting phrase or expression that sums up what your article is about, and use this as your title.

Editors sometimes change titles because they want one with more impact, but do try to find your own strong titles.

The less work the editor has to do on your article, the more favourably he will look upon you.

Look at the titles of travel articles already published in newspapers and magazines. Examine them carefully. What do they tell you about the article? Do they make you want to read on? And if so, why? Experiment with them for your own article. A title cannot be copyrighted. You can borrow the idea behind a title and express it in a different way.

Experiment with the following categories:
- Question: Why Do So Many People Go to Blackpool?
- How to: How to Enjoy Paris with Teenagers.
- Command: See Sweden this year!
- Alliterative: Beautiful, Bewitching Bali.

Rearrange proverbs and titles of books, use puns and quotations and anything else that you can turn into an interesting title. Study the titles of travel articles in those target markets you are aiming for and try to follow their format.

Remember that your title should be truthful as well as tempting. It should contain the angle of your article and not be so obscure that, although it may be very witty and clever, it gives no clue about what is to follow.

Ideas for titles are everywhere. Get into the habit of thinking about possible travel article ideas in terms of titles and jot them down in your notebook. For example, you may be writing about exploring Amsterdam's canals and as you wander around you notice how many taverns are scattered around the city. They are as traditional as the British pub and an essential part of Amsterdam life. Jot down a rough title like 'The Taverns of Amsterdam' in your notebook as a possible article. If you get into the habit of collecting titles you can build up a rich source of ideas.

The right style for the right market

Individual publications have their preferred styles and if you hope to sell your travel articles to them you should be aware of what their style is.

Study some articles in the travel sections of your target markets. When you do your market analysis you will make note of the style – as discussed in Chapter 5. Adapt your own style to that of your target market and always keep the reader in mind. Know who you are writing for.

I said earlier that style is the manner in which a writer expresses his or her individuality. By suggesting that you adapt your style to your target market I do not necessarily mean that you should, chameleon-like, change your style completely to suit each publication. You can still retain your individuality in the way you choose and arrange words and express opinions. Your own style will still show whether you write in the first person or third person, short or long sentences and paragraphs, elaborate or simple descriptions, or write for newspapers or magazines.

In time, you will find yourself gravitating toward those magazines and newspapers which reflect your own attitudes and points of view, but in the meantime you need to get as much published as possible, so consider the style of your target publication and use that as your guideline. Think of it as a canvas on which you are about to paint a picture. The size and shape of the canvas is decided for you but you are the one who creates the scene that will attract the viewer.

Look at the following examples of style, all quite different and unique in their way.

The first is the opening paragraph of a piece by Nicholas Gordon on Club Med, which appeared in the *Mail on Sunday*:

Crazy Sign Time. Somewhere between ten and 11, not East Caribbean Time, but Club Med Time, Crazy Sign Time. 'Are you ready, you GMs?' This is the Chef du Village, Mr Hansel Moss, five foot eight or thereabouts in his built-up boots, clutching a mike and looking like Mike Tyson. His hair is flat and smooth enough to land an F1–11 on.

Further down the column another paragraph:

Club Med is for doers. Oh, yes, when you arrive, it is made perfectly clear that this is your holiday and you can do as you wish, or not do as you wish. Clear? Good. But give yourself 24 hours and you discover that taking part *is* what you wish. Clear? Good.

Next, look at a travel article in *Vogue* by Rebecca Willis on unusual properties holidaymakers can rent across Britain:

An Englishman's summer home is someone else's castle. Or their mill, mansion, manorhouse, gatehouse, oast-house, abbey, water tower, game lodge or chapel. There are, of course, lots of reasons for renting abroad – not least, to borrow from Byron, 'The English winter ending in July/To recommence in August'. But since we somehow manage, in the face of all statistics, to remain optimistic about the weather, this does not, so to speak, cut any ice. Today there is more reason than ever for staying within these shores: the great British tradition of eccentricity, immortalized in bricks and mortar, is up for rent.

Lastly, a piece on Andalucia in *Bella*, by Barbara Jeffrey:

Malaga is one of the best-served airports in the Mediterranean for cheap charter flights, delivering holiday-makers to the glittering international resorts of Costa del Sol.

But it is also the gateway to another Spain – the ancient Moorish cities of Andalucia, with their mazes of narrow alleys, brilliant white houses festooned with geraniums and ornate wrought iron gateways giving tantalising glimpses of secret patio gardens. So, if you are planning an autumn break on the Costa del Sol, this is the ideal time to explore inland.

Seville, Granada and Cordoba are all easily reached by car, bus or train from Malaga which is a charming town, often ignored in the rush to the beaches. The once-scruffy alleys have been re-paved and the shops are packed with good-quality leather goods, especially shoes and boots, at half British prices.

These are three very different publications with three very different styles. In the *Mail on Sunday* article the style is snappy, staccato. It suggests that the reader is in for an action-packed holiday. Note that this style reflects the point of view of the article.

In the second example, the *Vogue* article, the style is more leisurely, the sentences longer; the piece contains a literary reference and, again, it suits the angle – a holiday spent in an abbey, oast house or chapel would surely be full of quiet country walks and peaceful hours with a good book.

The *Bella* extract is factual and to the point. It tells the reader he or she can fly via a cheap charter flight, describes the area and gives advice on what to buy. It is a straight-forward piece on how to get there, what to see, and how much it costs. And the style is exactly right for this type of article.

If, as suggested in Chapter 5, you have selected three or four target markets, look at the travel articles and place them side by side. Read them carefully. Make notes on the style and when you submit your work to the publications make sure you have observed their ground rules – that you have used the same size and shape of canvas.

Remember your reader profile, and always write with this person in mind.

Books on style

Waterhouse on Newspaper Style, by Keith Waterhouse, (Viking, 1989). This is a gem of a book. Not only is it a very good introduction to the use of language in today's newspapers, it is also an enjoyable, entertaining read.

This book was originally conceived as an in-house handbook for the *Daily Mirror*. Although it is described as the manual of tabloid journalism it will be helpful to any writer for any kind of publication. After reading this you will never again use a cliché – such as 'Dream Holiday' – or smother your work in 'a ketchup of adjectives'.

The Elements of Style, William Strunk Jr & E. B. White, MacMillan Publishing Co. Inc., New York, 3rd Edition, 1979. An excellent book, concise and readable, and tells you everything you need to know about style in a slim volume of 85 pages.

Browse around in the reference section of a good bookshop. There are many books on how to write and many contain sections on style.

MARKETING (3) – SELLING

Selling your travel articles to an editor can take as much time, skill and energy as it does to write them – sometimes more. For the new writer this can be daunting but careful market research and knowledge of who you are writing for will put you on the right track.

Approaching editors

Travel editors are busy people; they have a page to fill every week or month and they have to defend the pieces they have chosen in regular editorial meetings where other editors of other pages are doing exactly the same thing. The decision is not theirs alone – they too have a boss, and if they don't put forward material that readers want, they are in trouble. Of course, they are experienced and know what the needs of the magazine are, but they are still under pressure to come up with ideas that are fresh and interesting. They are waiting to hear from *you*.

They probably have a pile of quite unsuitable travel articles on their desk, sent in by hopeful newcomers who have obviously not studied the style or readership of their publication, who have addressed their covering letter to a travel editor who left over a year ago, and whose manuscript looks as though it was typed by the family dog. These are the articles which immediately go into the box to be returned with a short 'Thanks, but no thanks' note.

Another way to decrease your chances of impressing the editor is to telephone her with a vague idea for a travel piece and expect her to discuss it with you. Don't expect any travel editor to feed you ideas – if you have not got a sharp, interesting angle you should wait until you do. And don't irritate her with calls like the following:

'Hello, I'm John Brown. I wondered if you would like a travel article on China, I shall be going there next month.'

Stifled yawn. 'What exactly are you going to write about?'

If you can't come up with an interesting idea you have wasted her time and your own, as well as having left her with an unfavourable impression.

At this stage in your writing career it is probably better not to telephone travel editors at all, although there are occasions when it is appropriate to telephone – more about this later.

Most editors are reluctant to assign articles to unknown writers, especially over the telephone; there are better and more efficient ways of introducing yourself and your work.

The query letter

One of the main differences between amateur and professional freelance writers is that the beginning writer will write his article first and then try to sell it, whereas the experienced writer sells his work *before* writing it. For the person who is trying to make a living from travel writing, to spend hours writing and researching an article, without any assurance that he will be paid for doing so, is the quickest route to the dole queue. Professional travel writers rarely write articles without first getting the go-ahead from an editor.

That's all very well for experienced writers, you might say, but what about me? Editors don't know me from Adam, why should they give me a commission?

The best route to getting to know editors and to getting your work published is via the letter of enquiry, or query letter. Here's how it works.

The query letter represents your initial approach to the editor; it offers you your best chance for a good sales pitch. If you can describe your idea briefly and concisely in well-written prose and show the editor why it is right for his readers, you are halfway to success. Travel editors are always looking for new ideas and they would much prefer to receive well-thought-out query letters than manuscripts which, although they may be interesting and well written, cover either topics they have lined up for future issues or ones that appeared six months previously.

Another advantage of the query letter is that it not only sells an idea but also sells *you* as the person to write about it. It takes time to write a good query letter but I guarantee it will pay off in the long run. Spend as much time composing your query as you would on the opening paragraph of the article itself. Remember how important it is to 'hook' the reader with an interesting opening. One way of achieving this is to actually write the opening paragraph of your article and use this in your query letter. For example, the following is the beginning of an article I wrote on stately homes:

Events that changed the course of history have taken place in them. The great and the not-so-great have lived in them. Painted and photographed, admired and abused, they have survived the centuries. As Noel Coward said, 'We'll stand by the Stately Homes of

England', and with any luck we'll be standing by them for centuries to come.

For the query letter I added:

Millions of people visit Britain's castles and stately homes every year. There are hundreds of them scattered across the length and breadth of the country, but how do you decide which to see? It's not easy.

This article will help your readers decide what they want to see and how best to see it. I will include information on how to find organised tours and how to 'do-it-yourself'. I will also provide anecdotes and historic background information.

This query resulted in a commission from the editor.

Putting the effort into composing a good first paragraph that you can use in your query letter forces you to think clearly about how you are going to write your article. Often travel writers have what seems like a great idea but when they come actually to write about it they find either they don't know enough or there isn't enough material to make it an interesting story. Once you have written your carefully considered query, and the editor expresses interest, all you have to do is deliver what you promised. You've already done the groundwork.

Better than sending one good idea to an editor is to send two or three, especially if you are approaching a publication for the first time. This not only shows that you are capable of coming up with more than one idea, but also that – if each idea is sharp and interesting – you are a person who can write.

There are a few things you should consider when writing your query letter:

Don't include too much information – this is one of the

most common errors. Remember that you are enticing the editor with your idea, and you want her to be curious about what else you have to say. Don't give everything away in the initial approach – leave some surprises.

Do limit your query to one page. If you cannot describe your idea briefly you may have trouble in writing the final piece because you probably have not thought it through clearly enough. Also, a one-page query looks better and is more likely to be read: an editor can quickly glance over a page to see if it contains anything of interest, whereas she may put anything longer in her tray to be dealt with later – and that could take weeks. Figure 7.1 is an example of a query letter I wrote to a newspaper in the United States and which resulted in a sale. The editor asked to see the piece on canals and bought it.

Do mention any particular qualifications you might have for writing this article, i.e. did you spend a year in Tibet or were you a safari guide in Africa? If you have no specific expertise don't worry about it – your piece will have to stand on its own feet anyway – but if you have, mention it.

You should also tell the editor about any travel articles you have published before. If all you have had in print appeared in the school magazine or the *Church Times*, say nothing. What you are trying to do with your query letter is present yourself in the best possible light, so tell the editor of previously published work only if it was printed in a professionally produced publication and you were paid for it.

Some editors ask to see copies of previously published work if they are approached by a writer they don't know. This is a Catch-22 situation. How do you get experience without getting experience? All you can do at this stage is be honest. Do not say anything in your initial letter about never having been published before. Be confident in your approach and give the editor the impression that if given the job, you can do it.

Your address
Date

Mary Jones,
Travel Editor,
Name of Publication,
Address.

Dear Ms. Jones,

Are you interested in either of the following ideas for XXXXX?

CANAL WALKING IN LONDON

Beneath the bustling life of Britain's capital city is a secret peaceful world of canals which swing in a wide arc through the heart of London. It's a fascinating world to explore. The canals wander between factories and warehouses, opening out into parks, gardens, and nature reserves, providing unusual views of some of London's best-known landmarks.

It is possible to walk along the greater part of London's fifty-four miles of towing paths, and most of the access points are close to bus routes or underground stations – making the canals ideal for short strolls or longer rambles. There is an abundance of plants and waterbirds in a setting not only ideal for walking but also for photography, sketching, or just relaxing in the numerous canalside pubs and restaurants.

I will give historical information, anecdotes, and clear instructions on how to proceed.

ANTIQUE MARKETS OF LONDON

London has dozens of antique markets selling everything from bric-a-brac to pieces worth thousands of pounds, and there is little you can't find if you look hard enough. Prices are often below those of shops and stores, where overheads can lead to a big mark-up. There are bargains to be had for those willing to rise early and get there when the dealers arrive – the best buys are snapped up early. For example, at Bermondsey Market serious buyers and dealers arrive at 4 a.m. to scan the stalls (with torches in winter). But for the less ardent there's still plenty to choose from at the more civilised hour of 9:30 a.m. or so.

I shall select some of the best and most interesting markets and describe what they specialise in and what prices are like.

I have published numerous travel articles and can supply good-quality 35 mm colour transparencies. I look forward to hearing from you.

Yours sincerely,

Figure 7.1. Example of query letter

'On spec' and unsolicited manuscripts

An editor is unlikely to commission a travel piece from you if she knows nothing about you or the quality of your work, but if your query letter has sparked an interest she will probably ask you to send in your article 'on-spec'.

'Spec' is short for 'speculation': one definition the dictionary gives is 'a risky transaction'. In this situation the risks are taken by the writer; he has to spend time and energy in writing the article without any promise of acceptance, while the editor is risking nothing. However, if you are asked to submit a travel piece on spec, do so, and regard this as a sign of encouragement. This means that the editor likes your idea and will be prepared to take a serious look at your article. If you send in an interesting, well-written and carefully researched piece of work you stand a good chance of it being accepted.

Editors are often financially strapped and cannot afford to take chances on unproven writers. Unless they know your work they can hardly be expected to promise to pay for something that may turn out to be quite unsuitable. Therefore they protect themselves by asking for work on spec.

If you send an article to an editor who has not requested it, the manuscript is 'unsolicited'. It is possible to break into print in this way and this is the route most favoured by many new writers. However, in order to sell an unsolicited travel article you will need to have targeted your market very carefully and to be aware of which travel destinations have been covered over the past year in the publication.

By sending out completed manuscripts one at a time to various magazines you are greatly slowing down your chances of publication. Why? Because an editor may hold on to your article for weeks, sometimes months, before returning it. This means that one travel piece may be seen by only four of five editors during the course of a year, whereas you could send out twenty or thirty query letters over the same period of time. Also, if you have carefully targeted your articles to specific publications you will have to do some rethinking, and rewriting, in order to submit them elsewhere. All very time-consuming and unnecessary.

Even if you were very prolific and produced one travel article each month – and when would you find time for travelling? – you would have only twelve articles per year. Whereas if you sent query letters, with two or three ideas in each, you could have three or four times that number in circulation. Another consideration is expense: if you want your unsolicited manuscript to be returned you must always enclose a stamped, addressed envelope. This doubles the cost of postage. I don't enclose a s.a.e. with a query letter as I find most editors telephone if they are interested in my ideas, and those who are not interested usually send a standard rejection note or a short letter saying why they are not suitable.

Some publications will not consider unsolicited manuscripts and say so in the *Writers' & Artists' Yearbook* and *The Writer's Handbook*. So do check first and save yourself time and money.

In most cases I would suggest you query travel editors rather than submitting complete manuscripts. There are, however, occasions when you might send the finished product.

If, for instance, you have already spent a lot of time writing up an article for a specific publication – perhaps the editor asked for it on spec and then turned it down – it may be worthwhile for you to do some rewriting, reshaping and retargeting, and send if off somewhere else. I suggest this because I know how disappointing it is to put a lot of work into an article and then have it returned, only to gather dust on your desk for months.

A travel article which has already been sold in this country might be suitable for a similar publication abroad. For example, if you have sold a piece to *The Adventurers*, a British travel magazine which wants first-person accounts of off-beat places, preferably at a distance from venues frequented by tourists, you could try to sell it again to a publication such as *Real Travel*, a Canadian magazine which publishes articles 'for the adventure traveller' on untouched corners of the globe. (More about selling to overseas markets in Chapter 9.) Since the piece is already written you have nothing to lose by trying it with another magazine, but don't forget your market research – you must make sure you are sending your article to an appropriate publication.

Presentation and layout

A neatly typed and well laid out manuscript will not guarantee its acceptance but if you send in a sloppily presented article, with miserly margins, typed on paper that is too thin and with ribbons pale and worn out, it may never be read at all. The better it looks the easier it is to read and the better the impression you will make on the editor, so put as much care into the presentation of your manuscript as you have into its creation.

Your article should be typed on A4 white bond, 60–80 gms weight for the top copy and bank paper or onionskin for copies. Always use double spacing to allow for corrections made to your text by sub-editors. Right and left margins are used for instructions to the printers so leave plenty of room. Allow 1½" for the left-hand margin and 1" for the right, top and bottom margins.

Type on one side of the paper only and use a paperclip to hold pages together. Pages should be numbered in the top right-hand corner and you can let the editor know there are more pages by typing 'more' or 'M/F' (more follows) at the bottom.

At the top left-hand corner of each page type an abbreviated version of your article's title, i.e. for 'Exploring the Greek Islands' type 'Greek Islands'. This is sometimes called a catchline and is helpful if pages of your manuscript become detached.

The first page of your article should contain your name and address and the number of words. Centre your title about a third of the way down the page, move two spaces down and type 'by' and centre your name two spaces below that. See Fig. 7.2.

Underlining tells the printer that you want that word italicised, so do not underline any words unless this is what you want.

Do not leave the first line of a paragraph sitting by itself at the bottom of a page – start the paragraph on the next page.

Do not use fancy typefaces such as italics or script. Editors prefer pica (ten characters per inch) or elite (12 characters per inch). For manuscripts of more than three pages I type up a title page. See Fig. 7.3.

If you are sending an unsolicited manuscript or one that is on spec, and you wish it to be returned, remember to enclose a stamped, addressed envelope.

Articles less than six or seven pages in length can be folded in two and sent in an A5 envelope. Longer manuscripts should go into A4 envelopes.

Produce a clean, professional-looking manuscript that indicates your pride in your work and you will create that all-important good first impression.

HOW TO WRITE AND SELL TRAVEL ARTICLES

John Brown,   (1000 words on 5 pages)
20 High Street,
Your Town.
Tel: 000–111–222

EXPLORING THE GREEK ISLANDS
by
JOHN BROWN

Begin your article here, and for all subsequent paragraphs indent five
spaces.
          Like this.

Figure 7.2.
Example of first page of article

EXPLORING THE GREEK ISLANDS
by
JOHN BROWN

John Brown,
20 High Street,
Your Town.
Tel: 000–111–222
(1000 words on 5 pages)

Figure 7.3.
Example of Title Page

How long should you wait for a response?

New writers tend to start worrying if they don't receive a reply to their article submission or query letter within a week or so of sending it. The fact is that you must give an editor at least six to eight weeks before you start to panic. Many will reply quickly, but if they reply too quickly it is often with a rejection, so be patient, no news can sometimes be good news. If an editor is interested in your piece she may have to show it to other editors before finally being able to approve its acceptance – this all takes time.

If, however, you have had an article or a query with a publication for two months or so it is perfectly acceptable for you to give the editor a gentle nudge in the form of a telephone call or a short note. Don't be afraid that this will spark off a rejection. More often than not the editor will apologise for the delay and attend to your submission fairly quickly. Manuscripts and letters do get lost and as long as a reasonable amount of time has passed before you start nudging, few editors will take offence.

If you are waiting for a reply to a query letter, a business-like and tactful way to remind an editor is to make a copy of your copy of the original query letter and send it off with a note saying something to this effect: 'I am enclosing a copy of a query letter mailed to you on 15 March. Since I have not heard from you I wonder if you received it. I enclose a stamped addressed envelope for your reply and look forward to hearing from you.'

There is no reason why you should wait a long time for a reply to your query before sending it out to another editor. You could set your own deadline for replies, perhaps three or four weeks, and if you don't receive a reply, write else-where. What happens, you might ask, if both editors decide they want your article? You should be so lucky to have such a problem! However, if it does happen, accept the best offer and write a polite letter to the other editor explaining what happened. Any editor worth his or her salt will realise that these things sometimes happen, and would not hold it against you next time you submit an idea to them – it may even encourage them to reply more quickly.

If you have sent an editor a complete manuscript rather than a query letter, and have waited two months or so for a response, you can either telephone the editor (or, preferably, her secretary) and ask if your article was received. I have done this many times and have always been treated with courtesy and told what is happening with my manuscript, which could be any of the following: a) they never received it – in which case send another copy; b) the editor has been on holiday and only just returned – they will get back to you very shortly; c) they are sorry, but it is not suitable; d) they want to buy it and were just about to write to you. I have had all of these responses from time to time, and have always found it worthwhile to follow up on an article that has been out for a while.

If you have to make expensive long-distance phone calls to editors you may prefer to run off another copy of your article and resubmit with a covering note indicating when the original was sent. If you still don't hear in about a month I should put a black mark against this particular publication, cross it off your list of target markets, and submit your article elsewhere.

Getting paid

No matter how anxious you are to see your travel articles in print you must see to it that you get paid for your work. If an editor accepts your article she is not doing you a favour and you do not need to feel grateful. Nor do you need to be embarrassed at the thought of discussing money. Getting paid for a job well done is the mark of the professional and if your travel article is good enough to be accepted it is certainly good enough to be paid for. Remember what Dr Johnson said, and don't be a blockhead.

Rates of pay are usually quoted as so many pounds per thousand words and the amount can vary greatly between different publications. At the time of writing the *Lady* pays £55 per 1,000 words, whereas *Good Holiday Magazine* pays £150 per 1,000 words. Quite a difference.

Consult the *Writers' & Artists' Yearbook* or *The Writer's Handbook* for the current rates.

The National Union of Journalists will give you information on freelance rates but you should remember that these rates apply only to those freelances who are members of the NUJ. As a beginning writer you will hardly be able to demand union rates but it may be helpful for you to have an idea of what the going rates are. The amount quoted by the NUJ is always a minimum rate – many publications pay much more than this.

In the early stages of getting into print it is important for you to get some travel articles published and to begin to build up a portfolio of work, which will give you more credibility when you tackle new publications. At this point I don't think you should try to strike hard bargains with editors over the amount you will be paid. But you should determine exactly how much you will be paid and when you will get the money. You will either be paid on acceptance or on publication.

Payment on acceptance means the editor will pay you as soon as she accepts your travel article for publication. This is of course the best way to be paid. Even if your article never gets published – the editor could decide not to use it after all – you will receive a cheque for the work you have done. Most professional travel writers insist on this arrangement.

Payment on publication means exactly that. The writer receives no money for his or her article until it has been printed in the magazine that accepted it. It also means that you could (as I have) wait a year or more before you receive a cheque or see your article published. Travel editors often have a stockpile of articles and the piece you submit in January could easily be filed away until December. Payment on publication carries the risk that you may not get paid at all if the editor changes her mind about using your article, but if you want to get published you have to take this risk.

Holding on to markets

The happy day has arrived – you have had your first travel article accepted and you can't wait to see it in print. Please do not wait until it *is* in print before you approach the editor with more ideas. You now have an important contact and you should do your best to maintain it. Do not let the editor forget you. Once you have sold a piece to a publication follow it up as quickly as possible. Write to the editor, remind her that she has just bought a travel article from you and you are submitting further ideas for her consideration. Don't wait too long as she will forget you and probably will not remember your article either. All editors are keen to maintain contact with writers who can produce what they need, so don't feel shy about approaching an editor again soon after she has accepted work from you.

Once you have built up some rapport with an editor it is quite in order to telephone her with any ideas you may have, but make sure you have given them some thought and can express yourself clearly and succinctly. The busy editor does not have time for waffling.

8

PICTURES DOUBLE SALES

A picture is worth a thousand words. Put another way, a good picture can make a thousand words much more valuable.

What kind of pictures?

Your travel article stands a greater chance of publication if you can supply good photos. They will enhance your story and give the reader and editor a complete picture. Travel articles are sometimes accepted without pictures but if you can supply a package of both you will save the editor from spending time tracking down suitable pictures to accompany your article. You will also save him money, as paying a professional photographer or buying photos from a picture library will cost more than photos produced by the writer.

'Slides' and 'transparencies' are terms used synonymously when referring to positive colour film and these are used, and preferred, by most magazines. Make sure they are in sharp focus with good colour, without the orange or blue tinge that is often the result of bad processing.

Black and white film is usually referred to as 'negatives'. If you are planning to write mainly for newspapers this is what you should use. For good reproduction you will need to send the editor large glossy prints, at least 7″ by 5″. Many professional travel writers carry two cameras with them – one for transparencies and one for black and white.

Do not use colour prints to illustrate your travel article. They generally do not reproduce well and magazines that use colour photography almost always prefer transparencies.

When you do your market research note what kind of pictures are used. The *Lady*, for instance, always uses black and white although most magazines use colour. Note also the subject of the pictures. Family-oriented publications such as *Bella* or *Take a Break* like shots of people eating at outside cafés, playing on the beach or shopping in local markets, whereas *Vogue* often uses pictures of elegant buildings and romantic empty landscapes. In general, however, readers are interested in how other people live, work and play, and most publications prefer pictures with people in them.

Avoid photographic clichés as you would written ones. You don't need to take a picture of the Eiffel Tower to show the reader you are in Paris, or Big Ben if you are in London. Don't shoot the obvious scene; rather, you should take pictures of what you respond to yourself. If you follow your instinct and take shots of what captures your imagination and interest, the resultant pictures will probably do the same for the reader. If you must take a clichéd scene, try shooting it from an unusual angle.

How to get the best out of your film

Professional photographers usually take far more pictures than they need in order to get the best possible shot, so don't be stingy with film. It's cheaper to shoot a lot of film than it is to have duplicates made of your pictures, especially colour, and compared with the cost of getting to your destination in the first place, film is a minor expense. I take three or four shots of every scene, then if I want to write other articles about the same place I have enough pictures to accompany them. You can also get new ideas and different angles for travel pieces from the photographs you take, so keep an open mind when you shoot.

Try shooting your subject from different angles – from above and below or framed by branches or arches – and if there's a particular building you want to photograph, take it at different times of the day to capture the different effects of the light. Colour saturation is greatest during early morning and late afternoon and this is when lighting is most interesting. Avoid the harsh light of high noon.

With the selection of reasonably priced, fully automatic cameras on the market today, even the most inexperienced photographer can take saleable pictures. I know, I've done it. The secret is to keep it simple at first, and don't be too 'arty' or adventurous unless you really know what you are doing. You will want to send a varied selection of pictures with your travel article, so try for different effects. You can create a different impression of the same picture by taking both vertical and horizontal shots. Take shots of the overall scene, then take close-ups of details within that scene, such as handicrafts at a market stall, unusual road signs, statues, interesting bits of architecture.

When you take shots of people they should not be stiffly posed or looking at the camera. They will look more natural if you snap them when they are off their guard and perhaps engaged in some characteristic activity that relates to what you are writing about. Keep the background uncluttered and simple and get in as close to your subject as possible, filling the frame with him or her. Remember to have what is important in the frame and anything that doesn't matter outside of it. If you have your subject slap in the centre of the frame surrounded by empty space it weakens your image and makes him or her look unimportant. Some photographers say you should move in until you think you are close enough – then step another three feet closer.

Many a good picture is ruined by a camera strap or a finger being in the way, so make sure you really look at what is in the viewfinder and don't take shots of ugly telegraph wires or a tree growing out of someone's head.

Before going on your trip, replace batteries in your camera and take a plentiful supply of film – it often costs more at popular tourist resorts and in out-of-the-way places you often cannot buy it at all.

Other sources of photographs

Photographs will help sell your article, but what do you do if your one and only set of pictures get spoilt or lost, it rains every day of your holiday, or you haven't got a camera and can't afford to buy one? Don't despair, there are many sources from which you can obtain good quality travel pictures.

Tourist offices want you to draw attention to their country and will supply pictures free of charge. You may be required to sign for them and be asked to pay a small sum if they are lost or damaged. If you borrow transparencies make sure they are in good condition, with good colour and sharp focus. Don't use them if they are not good enough.

Scour junk shops and jumble sales for old books and magazines. Fifty years after the death of the author/artist/photographer they are out of copyright and you are free to use them. But to be on the safe side I would allow eighty to ninety years. Many old engravings are fascinating and would provide interesting illustrations for travel articles. If you don't want to tear out the page you could send a good quality photocopy.

Some antiquarian bookshops have boxes of old postcards. An article on Brighton, for instance, illustrated with pictures of how it looked in the 1920s, might catch an editor's interest.

Airlines, travel agencies and tour operators will often supply free photographs to travel writers as will the representatives at the World Travel Market held at Olympia, London, every year. If you do borrow photographs from such sources they should be stamped 'Copyright Free'.

There are dozens of picture libraries listed in the *Writers' & Artists' Yearbook* covering every country in the world and if you have trouble in getting the right kind of picture for your article you may want to contact one of these, but check around as this can be quite an expensive way of obtaining pictures.

If you absolutely cannot find suitable photographs or illustrations for your travel article, let the editor send out a professional photographer or contact the picture libraries himself. If he really wants your article the lack of photographs will not prevent him from publishing it.

When and how to send pictures

When you send your query letter to the editor, tell him you can supply photographs and say what kind they are – 35mm colour transparencies or black and white photographs. Unless you have a commission which includes photographs it is too risky to send pictures on spec, so do not send any photographs unless you have been asked to do so. They could sit around on the editor's desk for weeks before your article or query is read and it is not unknown for them to be lost, never to appear again. It is also expensive as slides and photographs should be sent by registered post and packed very carefully to prevent damage.

The editor has given you the green light; he likes your travel article and wants pictures. Take as much care with the presentation of your pictures as you do with your manuscript. Carefully labelled and captioned pictures will assist their safe return to you and will be helpful to the editor.

I send my colour transparencies in A4 page-sized plastic sheets which have little pockets into which each transparency can be fitted. There are twenty pockets to each page and I usually send between fifteen and twenty slides. This allows the editor a reasonable choice but is not so many as to confuse him. Remember that your pictures should complement the text of your travel article. If the subject is not mentioned in your story, don't send a picture just because it is one of your best shots.

Small name and address labels are ideal for sticking on to slides. The 1½″ × ½″ size is just about right. Each slide should have a caption and a number. You can type this information on to sticky labels and cut them to fit on to your slide. Number the slides in the order you want the editor to view them; this sequence should usually complement that in which the subject is mentioned in your article.

If you are sending black and white photographs, write your name and address in pencil on the back with a brief caption and a number. Do not press heavily – photographic paper is fragile and any marks showing through will spoil your picture. Felt pens can smear, so avoid using them. The best solution is to have a rubber stamp made with your name and address on it, and use this. It also comes in useful for stamping your address on envelopes or notes. Do not use paper clips which may damage the photos. Place them between pieces of stiff cardboard and secure them with an elastic band. I mail all my photos and slides in padded envelopes which offer good protection.

For both slides and photographs you should include a separate sheet with matching numbers and captions. If you have extra information about the pictures that will interest the editor, elaborate on the caption sheet. For instance, if you have included a picture with a close-up of a butterfly you might mention that this particular species of butterfly is found only in northern Spain.

What you can earn from your pictures

I used to work with a photographer who took the pictures for my articles, and I had to pay him a hefty chunk of my fee. Since I have begun to take my own pictures I have increased my income by a third. You can do the same. When I started I knew nothing about photography and my camera was a simple inexpensive model, but I took lots of pictures for each article and, with beginner's luck, there were usually a few that were good enough to submit. So don't be put off taking your own pictures; some very reasonably priced cameras today are practically foolproof and the more pictures you take the more experienced you become.

Payment for pictures varies greatly. I have received between £15 and £40 for the use of one transparency. A roll of film for colour slides, with 36 exposures, costs about £8 and this includes processing, so the sale of just one transparency at the low end of the pay scale will pay for 72 colour transparencies. Don't stint on film; just a few good shots will more than repay your initial costs.

There are other ways to make money from your travel pictures; the *Writers' and Artists' Yearbook* lists firms which are prepared to consider photographs for calendars and

113

postcards, and if you have some shots that are really outstanding you might want to sell *them* with just an accompanying paragraph.

Words from a professional photographer

Christine Osborne is a photojournalist who specialises in travel, food and culture, focusing on life in the Middle East and developing nations. She has fourteen published books and has her own photo-stock library on sixty countries. She has the following advice on travel photography:

'On learning I am a travel photographer, people immediately ask what camera I use, as if the camera is a magic key to making saleable pictures. They are usually pleased to hear that I work with moderately priced, yet strong and trustworthy equipment. Keep it simple is good advice – and I probably could not operate some of the complex cameras on the market today.

'I quickly learned a camera was essential when I became a travel writer in the early 1970s. I bought a Pentax Spotmatic, the first featuring TTL (through the lens) metering in an SLR or single lens reflex camera. Today I use a Nikon – still manual, I hasten to add. Any good-brand camera can do the job because the picture that catches the eye is largely created by composition.

'If you are a first-time buyer, hunt down some classic cameras offered second hand. Some recommended models are the Spotmatic, Yashica FX-D, Canon EF and the Olympus Trip 35. They may take some finding, but try some reputable second-hand camera shops.

'If you are one of those people who would rather opt for a new camera, you should investigate one of the currently popular autofocus SLR's, ranging in price from £200 to

£2000. The alternative is a manual focus SLR of which there are dozens of models. Two good manual models are the Pentax K–1000 and the Praktica BX20. The price rises along with various metering systems, exposure modes and other gadgets. You can buy a Ricoh KR–10M, a Yashica 108MP and a Vivitar V6000 for less than £200, including the lens.

'The lens plays a vital role in producing a good photograph which can stand up to enlargement. There is no point in purchasing a good camera and clipping a cheap lens on it. You will get a similar result to photographing through a milk bottle.

'A 50mm lens used to be sold with the camera but this standard practice has been sensibly dropped. Today you can usually buy a camera body and decide what lens you prefer. You will soon learn from experience and personal taste. Many people who use autofocus opt for the 35–70mm zoom which is extremely versatile.

'A flash completes your travel photography outfit. Apart from night shots, it is useful for highlighting daytime shade. Instead of asking your subjects to look into the sun, have them stand with their backs to it and *flash them*. This cuts out the 'holiday squint' common in travel photography.

'Buying film is the cheapest part of travel photography, so do not skimp. Today, the nightmare of running out of film is largely transcended by the ubiquitous Fujichrome film which, or so it seems, is sold all over the world. If buying abroad, however, check the expiry date and try to ensure that the film has been stored in cool conditions. In a hot climate keep your film in good condition by asking if you can store it in the hotel refrigerator.

'The initial composition is the most important part of taking good travel photographs, or indeed any photograph. How you frame a picture is how you see the world. Some people have a natural talent for composition and can create a striking image without even thinking about it, but most of us need to learn a few simple rules in order to take successful pictures.

'If you are taking a picture of a house, for example, the result will be more interesting if you place it in the left-hand third of the picture, rather than bang in the centre. And when taking pictures of groups – be they people, donkeys, or anything else – an odd number tends to be more eye-catching than an even number.

'Remember to depict your subject upright as well as horizontal, as art directors like a choice. They do not, however, like to see dozens of different shots of the same subject, so submit your six best. You will be dearly loved if you have left space in an upright photo for the magazine title, or logo – a cover picture being every travel photographer's dream. Some publications pay up to £700 – enough to send you around the world again.'

9

SELLING OVERSEAS

Throughout this book a strong emphasis has been placed on the importance of proper market research, and this is equally true for the overseas market. In the UK you can go into any well-stocked bookshop and browse through the magazine rack, taking note of the best markets for travel articles and perhaps buying one or two magazines to study in greater depth. With overseas publications this is obviously not so easy, although some large bookshops do stock a few foreign magazines. However, there's nothing quite as reliable as studying a publication at first hand, and you can build up a profile of an overseas publication in a number of ways.

How to find overseas markets

To become familiar with the overseas market you can study the foreign newspaper and magazine listings in the *Writers' & Artists' Yearbook* as well as various marketing publications that are available. For example, *Freelance Market News* always has an overseas supplement. At the time of writing, the latest edition gives the requirements of magazines in the United States and Australia. Other supplements have covered markets in the Far East, Europe and Canada and they give guidance on editors' requirements, length of article and rate of pay. In general, the publications listed are not specifically for travel articles but some list travel in their editorial requirements and should be added to your target markets.

Writers News and *Writers' Monthly* are also good sources of foreign market information. And don't forget the reference library, where you can scour the pages of *Benn's Press Directory* for details of thousands of publications around the world, and *Willing's Press Guide* which gives the principal publications of Australasia, the Americas and Europe.

Some overseas magazines will send you sample copies, although you may in some cases have to send a money order to cover the cost and the postage. Many will send you their writer's guidelines. These are invaluable, as they tell you exactly what the editor is looking for. Collect as many of these as you can; you will find them enormously helpful when searching for new markets for your travel articles.

You can also build up your collection of foreign publications by checking out the newspaper kiosks and bookshops when you are abroad. And don't forget the in-flight magazines. Every airline has its own magazine and they provide a good market for the freelance travel writer.

Ask your travelling friends to bring back local publications for you and if you have relatives or friends living abroad put them to work too. Foreign embassies and high commissions often have reading rooms where you can study newspapers and magazines.

If all this seems like hard work, it's worth it – as you will see when those cheques in dollars, francs and lire start coming in.

Selling your work many times

The hard work you have put into writing your travel article pays off when you receive your cheque and see your story in print. But that need not be the end of it – you can collect several cheques for the same article by selling it to overseas publications. The beauty of this is that you need to do very little extra work – the research is already done, the piece is written, and it can be used again and again to increase your income and widen your audience.

This is perfectly legal. What you are selling is the *right* for a publication to use your work, and you can sell that right repeatedly. More about 'rights' later in this chapter.

At this point you might be asking, 'What about target marketing?' Proper market research is, as always, very important, but once you have become familiar with the requirements of overseas publications by doing as I have suggested above, you will be able to pick up on the general tone of each magazine. For instance, the Australian magazine *Holiday & Travel News* is described in *Freelance Market News* as a glossy travel magazine containing features such as 'Graz – Austria's Second Largest City'; 'Zakopane – Poland's Ski Capital', and an article on the Irish links of Prince Edward Island. From this it would seem that *Holiday & Travel News* covers a variety of destinations and likes travel articles with a specific angle. If you have a published piece that you think might suit this magazine, send off a query letter to the editor. This is how I approach a new overseas market; I am often asked to send in the piece on spec, usually resulting in a sale.

At this stage, if asked to submit the article on spec, I usually send it as is, and have sold many pieces without having to make any changes at all. If the editor likes your travel article, and there are only slight stylistic alterations to be made, she will take it and change it accordingly. If she loves the idea but stylistically it needs a lot of work, she may ask you to write it in a lighter, more chatty style, reduce it from 1,500 words to 1,000, or include more information on hotel prices, etc. All you have to lose is the cost of the postage, so take a chance and start sending out those query letters. You have already been paid for the article once – anything else you earn is icing on the cake.

Some travel articles will have a broader appeal than others. For example, if you wrote a piece on 'The Joys of Travelling Alone' or 'How to Survive Jet Lag', you would be covering topics of interest to travellers everywhere. But if you wrote articles on something particularly British, such as 'Following Wainwright Along the Pennine Way' or 'Exploring Durham – Land of the Prince Bishops', you might find such topics don't cross foreign borders that easily. Both overseas and British travel articles, however, will sell to English-language publications in foreign countries providing you put some careful thought into where you are sending them.

Once you have tapped into the overseas market you will not find it difficult to discover new outlets for your travel articles.

How to approach overseas editors

It is too expensive to send articles by airmail if there is no guarantee that editors will be interested in them. A query letter will facilitate a quick reply, whereas your manuscript may lie in an in-tray until the editor has time to read it. This takes valuable time you could spend contacting other publications in the same country. If you want to reap the full benefits of selling to overseas markets, you should try to have as many articles in circulation as possible.

When you send query letters don't for🮤 🮤🮤🮤 🮤🮤 🮤🮤🮤 🮤🮤🮤 🮤 copy of their writer's guidelines. Offer to sen🮤 🮤🮤🮤🮤 🮤🮤🮤🮤 🮤🮤 🮤🮤🮤 lished work if required, and mention wheth🮤🮤 🮤🮤🮤 🮤🮤🮤🮤 photographs or transparencies to go with your a🮤🮤🮤🮤 🮤🮤 🮤🮤 also to your advantage to offer two or three ideas 🮤🮤 🮤🮤🮤🮤 query letter, as discussed in Chapter 7. Since you u🮤🮤🮤ly will not have a copy of the publication your market research cannot be as accurate, so giving the editor a few ideas greatly increases your chances of hitting the target.

In your initial query letter you can ask for a sample copy of the magazine, but I have found that very few editors respond to this. What generally happens is that they send me a copy only when they are interested in what I have to offer.

Many writers enclose with their query letter a self-addressed envelope and international reply coupons, which can be purchased at any post office, on the assumption that this will guarantee a reply. This is not always the case – some editors just don't bother to reply if they are not interested in your query. I no longer send international reply coupons with my queries and this has never prevented an editor from responding if she is interested in my ideas. It's not too much to expect a publication to cover the price of an airmail stamp for a letter, but it is absolutely necessary to include return postage costs if you are sending manuscripts and/or photographs which you want to be returned to you. I would, however, strongly advise you to send query letters rather than manuscripts. You may end up spending a lot of money on postage before making a sale.

If you have a word processor and can therefore dash off fresh copies of your work at the drop of a hat, and you really do want to send your manuscripts rather than query letters, you can ask the editor to dispose of the article if she is not interested in it. There have been occasions when I have done this, usually when I felt an article was just right for a specific publication and consequently decided to bypass the query letter step and take a chance on the manuscript. In such instances I include a self-addressed postcard with international reply coupons attached, requesting the editor to jot down a few words in reply.

Tackling the overseas market can sometimes assume a rather hit-and-miss aspect, but the odds that you will strike lucky are quite high and it is certainly worth taking a chance. I have sold many articles in this way and have gone on to write more pieces for the magazines I originally contacted. You will eventually receive copies of the issue in which your article appears and in time will manage to build up a reasonable collection of overseas contacts.

What to write about and how to write it

Most overseas travel publications are interested in articles about Britain. We live in a country rich in history and pageant and visitors from all over the world come here to explore the countryside, visit museums, gardens, stately homes, and historic sites. All this, and much more, provides material for the travel writer.

The American market is a big attraction for the freelance travel writer. Many of the bigger magazines pay fees much higher than anything you could get in this country. *Travel & Leisure*, for example, pays between 50 cents and $1.50 per word – at current rates of exchange that works out to approximately £285 to £860 per thousand words. But competition is stiff and a market such as this is very difficult to break into. However, there are hundreds of other American publications which pay well – even if not quite as well as *Travel & Leisure* – and they are certainly worth a try.

When writing for foreign markets, read your article over

carefully before sending it. Are there references to typically British events that may mean nothing to a foreign reader? Look out for slang and local expressions and, if writing for the American market, use American spelling whenever possible. You can buy books on American spelling at some of the larger bookshops.

Foreign stories as well as British ones will sell to overseas markets. If you have a new slant on the Costa del Sol or can present a fresh view of Naples, foreign readers will be interested in hearing about it. If you can find something that ties in with their culture you will have an even better chance of acceptance. Historical American connections with Britain abound, but what about Chinese culture in Paris? This could sell to a magazine in the Far East. You could investigate your local area to see if there are any foreign connections; perhaps an Australian TV or film star once lived, or lives, nearby. You could write something like 'What Jason Donovan Likes About The British Countryside', or 'Crocodile Dundee's Favourite Town', and try to sell this to an Australian newspaper or magazine.

Once you start thinking along these lines you will be surprised at how often you can find a foreign link.

It is, of course, not necessary to make such connections. If you know your area well and can write an article with broad appeal, it will be of interest to overseas readers as well as those closer to home.

Stories of adventure have wide appeal; even if readers have no intention of following in your footsteps they like to know how you do it, what happened on the journey, and what the country was like. So if you have climbed Everest, trekked in the Himalayas or travelled the Amazon, there is a world of readers waiting for your story.

English-speaking countries such as the USA, Canada, New Zealand, Australia and South Africa are obvious overseas markets to tackle and many other countries have

English-language magazines and newspapers. A few for you to think about are: Hong Kong, Japan, Pakistan, Singapore, the Philippines, Indonesia, Kenya and the Netherlands. There are many more, which you will discover as you continue to explore new markets for your travel articles.

Sending work overseas

I like the security of knowing that my article and precious transparencies are travelling by the safest route, and always send them by registered post, airmail. This can be expensive but is the most reliable way to send work overseas.

Do not use stick-on labels on packages that are to be registered. My local post office tells me this is to safeguard against someone sticking a label on your package with another address on it – in other words, redirecting it to themselves in the hope that there is something of value inside. So write the name and address directly on to the envelope.

Preparation and posting of photographs to overseas editors is the same procedure as that described in Chapter 8 under 'When and how to send pictures'.

Be sure to keep the Certificate of Posting which you will be given when you register your package. If it were lost en route this is proof that you did send it. I type 'Sent by registered airmail' at the top of the accompanying letter and staple the Certificate of Posting to my copy of the letter. I also write on the copy letter the cost of postage. I find this helpful when calculating what I am spending on sending work overseas. One or two sales will more than compensate for the cost of postage.

Getting paid

Once you start selling to the overseas market you will need to develop the art of patience. When it comes to getting paid there is often a long wait. Most editors pay on publication and there's never any guarantee as to when your travel article will actually appear. I have waited up to a year before receiving payment and seeing my piece in print. Nor does acceptance always guarantee publication; editors can change their minds and return your article to you neither paid for nor used. This does not happen very often but it is as well to be aware that it can happen.

If an editor has commissioned a travel article from you – either at home or overseas – and eventually decides not to use it, the very least you should receive is what is known as a 'kill' fee, so called because if it is not used it is, in effect, killed off. This can vary from 20 per cent to 50 per cent, depending on the policy of the publication. The matter of a kill fee is normally mentioned in the original commissioning letter, although it is not usual for editors to offer kill fees to writers they are using for the first time. However, I would suggest you be bold and ask for a kill fee if your work has been commissioned and then not used. This happened to me, with an overseas publication that was new to me. When the editor wrote to say she would not be using my article, I replied suggesting that I should receive a kill fee for the work I had done. Her answer was that she would use the article after all, if I would make some alterations to it. So I ended up with the full fee and my article in print. It pays to be assertive.

Any article that has been accepted, then turned down later, can be resubmitted elsewhere – even if you have received a kill fee.

If your economic survival depends upon receiving regular cheques for your travel articles, I would suggest you have as many pieces out as possible. You don't have to wait for payment before you submit another idea to the same publication. I often have two or three payments due to me from the same magazine. If you have cheques arriving regularly you will not be quite so upset over how long some of them take to reach you.

In this country, payment is generally described as being so many pounds per thousand words but many overseas publications quote their rates as being so much per word. One is not necessarily any better than the other – just a different way of doing business.

It's exciting when the cheques arrive, in envelopes with colourful foreign stamps, but bank charges on foreign exchange are high and if possible you should ask to be paid in sterling.

The business of rights

The new writer often finds talk about rights confusing, but there is actually little cause for bewilderment and if you are in the business of selling your work many times you need to know how you stand legally.

As a freelance travel writer you will mainly be concerned with two kinds of rights. 'Copyright' is one kind; 'All Rights', 'First Serial Rights' and 'Second Serial Rights' make up the other. (Here 'serial' means periodical. It is nothing to do with the serialisation of your work.)

Copyright is straightforward. When you create something, whether it is a painting, a novel, a sculpture or a travel article, you automatically own the copyright. This is the legal exclusive right which a person has to print, publish, and sell his own works, during a certain period of time – usually for the duration of the author's life and 50 years afterwards. Nobody else can copy your writing in exactly the same way – the right to copy is your copyright. Other writers may write about the same topic in a similar manner but they cannot copy exactly what you have written.

Ideas cannot be copyrighted, so if you see other travel articles on the same topic as yours, expressing the same point of view, there is nothing you can do about it. What copyright protects is the specific words you have used to express your idea, not the idea itself.

When you sell an article for the first time in a particular country you normally sell first serial rights. For example, if your travel article is making its debut in a British magazine, you would sell first British serial rights. This tells the editor that your article has not previously appeared in any British publication. The editor is buying the right to be the first to publish your article and you may not sell it to another British publication until it has appeared in print. Once it has been published you are free to sell second serial rights to another magazine. You will usually be paid less for second serial rights but it is a good way to generate more income from the same travel article.

Unless stated otherwise in your transactions with the editor, it is normally assumed that first British serial rights are being offered and there is no need to discuss this. Some writers type 'FBSR' in the top right-hand corner of the first page of their manuscript but it isn't necessary.

Although you cannot sell your article again in Britain until the magazine that bought first British serial rights has published it, you do have the right to sell it to a foreign magazine at the same time, in which case you would sell first North American rights, first Australian rights, etc. In such cases I always type the rights being offered on the manuscript. Some magazines never buy articles which have already been published, whereas others frequently do so, and it is also customary to indicate that the article has already been published in the UK.

Unless you are paid a whacking great fee you should, whenever possible, avoid selling all rights. To do so literally means giving up *all* rights to your work. The publication to which you have sold all rights can use your article again and again by selling it to other magazines, reproducing it in a book or re-using it at a later date. And you will not get a penny extra. Rights are not usually negotiated, so if you are asked to sell all rights, don't haggle. Get as large a fee as possible, rewrite your article, and sell it again as often as you can.

10

END PIECES

Even experienced writers are upset when they receive a rejection slip saying 'Sorry, but this does not fit our requirements at the present time.' And it's even more upsetting for the beginning writer who does not have the confidence of published work behind him.

Dealing with rejection

Rejections hurt but don't let them paralyse you. The important thing to bear in mind if you receive a rejection is that *it is just one editor's opinion*. It does not mean that your travel article was hackneyed, boring or badly written. What it does mean, in most cases, is that your piece was not right for that particular publication and, again, we come back to the importance of proper marketing. If you have received a go-ahead from an editor on the strength of a good query letter, your article can still be rejected if it does not fit the style and requirements of the magazine.

If you send travel articles in on spec and they are rejected, it is not always the case that there is something wrong with them. Sometimes a piece is rejected because the subject has already been covered, the editor is overstocked and can't take any more for the foreseeable future, or it is not the right time of year. This indicates, again, the importance of the query letter. If this is turned down all that is being rejected is the ideas you have proposed, not a complete piece of work that you have slaved over.

Some publications receive hundreds of travel articles and queries every week and editors are much too busy to explain why they are rejecting your work. Form rejection slips can often be very abrupt and sometimes convey a 'thanks, but no thanks' attitude. As a writer, you have to develop a thick skin and not let these get to you. If, on the other hand, the editor takes time to scribble a note on the rejection slip or, even better, writes a short letter saying why he didn't take your article, you should regard this as a definite sign of encouragement. If the editor really hasn't the slightest interest in your article, the easiest thing for him to do is to send a standard rejection slip. He doesn't have to think about it – into the envelope it goes. But, if he sees something of interest in your travel article, or likes your writing, he will often jot down a few words such as, 'Sorry, we can't use this, but try us again', or 'We used this destination last year, do you have more ideas?' This indicates he has noticed promise in your work and you *must* follow up on this. Respond immediately with more ideas or another suitable manuscript, thanking him for his note and words of encouragement.

If, however, you find the same travel article coming back to you time and again without comment, you should take another look at it. Are you sure you have targeted an appropriate market? Have you caught the right tone of the magazines you are approaching? Is your angle right for them? You must learn to recognise why it is being rejected.

Some of the best writers have had their share of rejections: *Watership Down* and *The Lord of the Rings* – both best sellers – were turned down time and time again.

Rudyard Kipling received a note from a publisher saying 'Sorry, but you just do not know how to use the English language', and George Orwell was told that 'it is impossible to sell animal stories'. So when you receive your next rejection note, remember that you are in good company.

Don't give yourself time to brood on the pain of rejection. With careful marketing you can have a string of possible outlets for your work. Check the next publication on your list and, when your article is rejected, send it out again immediately. Don't give up. As time goes on the disappointment gets less and if there is anything positive about receiving rejections it is that they show you are at least writing and sending work out – a certain path to publication.

Further sales

This same diligence should be applied to seeking different and unusual ways of selling your articles again and again. By being aware of the different ways by which you can recycle your work you can greatly increase your income.

When you consider the amount of time and expense that goes into writing a travel article – the cost of the holiday, time spent on research – you cannot afford to sell the article only once. Your basic research belongs to you, and you can use that research in many different ways to sell different articles to various publications. As you become more experienced as a travel writer you should be able to write at least three or four different articles about the same subject. Some of the same basic information will have to be repeated but you can tackle the subject from a different angle, make the beginnings and endings different, and change the title. For example, if you have written an article about a trip you made to New York you might produce articles such as 'Stroll

131

Around Central Park – It's Safer Than You Think', 'Night-life in Harlem', or 'New York for Kids'. Good research and copious notes will provide you with many spin-offs.

These spin-offs are new articles and can be sold accordingly – all rights, first serial rights, whatever you wish.

If you have previously published travel articles gathering dust in your filing cabinet, take them out and see how they can be updated. There's nothing new under the sun and most publications have a cyclical turnaround time for repeating the same subjects. It's a good idea to clip all relevant magazine and newspaper travel articles that have anything at all to do with a piece that you have written, and add them to your file. In time you will have masses of information that will help you to update your article. Places change, new tourist attractions are added, special charter flights are introduced – use all the information you can gather to make your old article fresh and timely.

Another way to get mileage out of previously published articles is to see if they have anything in common. For example, in a recent *Bella* travel article entitled 'Lovers in Paradise', Thailand, Jamaica, St Lucia, Seychelles and the USA were all compared for their romantic appeal to lovers and the availability of 'package' weddings. You could write an article on 'Places to Get Away from It All' or 'Holidays for the Adventurous'.

Be aware of what is happening in parts of the world that you have written about. Is there a significant anniversary coming up? Has a particular city received an accolade such as 'European City of Culture', or are there places about to celebrate their bicentenary, millennium, or whatever? Link up your old article with the new events and send it off, explaining to the editor the reason for its timeliness.

It takes time and creative thinking to find alternative outlets for your articles but it pays off, and it's fun!

Types of travel articles

There are many ways to write travel articles and the one
you choose will depend heavily on the market you are targeting. But, by being aware of the various forms in which
you can write your story you can increase your sales. Bear
this in mind when you do your initial research.

Personal experience

This type of travel article is the most popular with new
writers. And they usually want to tell *everything*. However,
if you can restrain yourself and choose a particular aspect
of your trip, there are many publications interested in this
kind of story. The national newspapers often publish personal experience travel articles, as do many of the more up-
market magazines.

When writing the personal experience piece remember
that the story you are telling, although personal, should be
of interest to an audience that does not know you and
really is not interested in the minutiae of your day-to-day
experience. If you had to wait a long time for the bus to
the next town or the restaurants served only black tea and
you wanted milk, don't elaborate on such things – I wouldn't
even mention them unless they have some relevance to the
story.

The reader wants to enjoy your trip through his own eyes;
he wants to experience the highlights, feel the hot sun, see
the strange sights. Give him the best – and the worst, if it
adds to the story – but do not give him a blow-by-blow
account of everything that happened.

133

Destination

This is the most commonly used type of travel piece. It tells the reader almost everything he needs to know about a particular destination, and your article should be packed with information on how to get there, where to stay, what to see, where to eat, nightlife, shopping, transportation – in short, *everything*.

Whereas the personal-experience article is often read by the armchair traveller who likes to experience travelling through someone else's eyes, the destination piece is intended for readers who want to go and are looking for good advice. Many will make up their minds about where to go on the strength of your article, so it must be as comprehensive as possible.

This does not mean, however, that your destination piece should be a boring list of things to do and see. It should be glued together with interesting historical anecdotes, descriptions of the geography, aspects of the culture that visitors should be aware of, and perhaps also a look at the political climate.

Humour

If you can see the funny side of situations and write about it, you will have editors lining up for your work. Humour is one of the most difficult kinds of writing, whether you are writing about travel or anything else, and editors just don't get enough. If you have an eye for the ridiculous, can laugh in the face of disaster, and are able to write about it, you have a huge audience waiting to hear from you. You would not need to target this type of article specifically at travel markets. A quick look at most newspapers and magazines will show that there is always room for humour.

134

If things go badly on your trip – say your 'ocean view' turns out to be two miles from the hotel; you lose your suitcase and you spend two days in a non-English-speaking town trying to replace basic essentials; or you stay in a hotel described as 'quaint' which turns out to be so primitive there isn't an iota of comfort in the place – turn your frustration around and look on the funny side. It's usually there somewhere!

Round-up

The article, 'Lovers in Paradise', described above, is an example of the round-up. This form is one of the most popular and the easiest to write, and the possibilities are endless. The round-up is essentially any kind of group that has something in common. It doesn't have to be places, it could be groups of celebrities: writers, pop stars, actors who are willing to name their favourite island, beach, hotel, airline – whatever you like as long as it has some connection with travel.

Other examples of the round-up could be articles on 'Holidays for the Disabled', 'The Six Best Stately Homes', or 'The Best Campsites in France'.

Round-ups that tell people how they can save money are also popular – for example, 'Parisian Restaurants You Can Afford', or 'London's Free Museums'.

A word about word processors

Recycling your travel articles will take less time and effort if you have a word processor; a fresh copy can be yours at the touch of a button, with no more 'white-out' corrections or painstaking retyping.

But the word processor is not only a tool for recycling articles. It can help the writer in many different ways and once you have mastered it you will wonder – as I do – how you ever managed without one.

Many writers who have not tried using word processors find the idea intimidating and fear that you have to be some kind of technological wizard to master them. Admittedly they may seem a bit daunting at first but the more you use them the easier it becomes. Don't allow yourself to be intimidated. Once you have the basic skills you will learn more sophisticated word-processing skills as you go along.

A word processor is essentially a specialised computer designed for writing, editing, and proofreading. It consists of three components: A keyboard which has the same layout as a typewriter, plus other command keys; a television-like screen which displays the material you have just typed in or retrieved from the machine's memory; and a printer which transfers material from the word processor into print.

For faster, more efficient writing you cannot beat a word processor. It makes editing easier by allowing you to read and correct your copy before you print it. It permits you to move paragraphs around within the text, and even counts words for you, and you can store dozens of articles in its memory and locate them instantly. If you are a poor speller it will even correct your mistakes as well as typographical errors. Many writers insist that using a word processor improves the quality of their writing. Since they don't have constantly to retype their articles they are able to spend more time on careful editing before submitting them.

Which word processor should you buy? This depends, as always, on what you can afford. The Amstrad PCW 8256, which came on to the market in 1985 at £399 (plus VAT) put word processors within the reach of most people who could afford a good electric typewriter. As technology improves and the market becomes more competitive, prices come down. At the time of writing I saw the Amstrad PCW 8256 advertised for £299 (plus VAT).

There are many types of word processor on the market and some of the newer, more expensive models are IBM compatible. The advantage of this is that typesetting today is largely done by computer, and the publisher's computer can read the discs from an IBM compatible system, thus saving a great deal of time and money for the publisher. However, many editors do not require a word processor to be IBM compatible and if you mainly intend to use yours for article writing I would suggest that a relatively inexpensive system, such as the Amstrad PCW 8256, would be more than adequate.

In computerspeak you may hear the word 'dot-matrix' bandied about. This is a term used to describe the printer that accompanies the word processor. A dot-matrix printer uses numerous small dots to form each letter of each word, making your work *look* as though a computer produced it – which of course it did. There is absolutely nothing wrong with this. I have heard that some editors will not accept dot-matrix printing, preferring instead letter-quality printers, which are much more expensive, but I have never come across one.

Dealing with the tax inspector

Whether you combine your travel writing with another job or you are a full-time freelance, you must disclose your earnings from writing at the end of the financial year. In other words, if you make any kind of profit from writing –

137

if your earnings are greater than your expenses – you must pay income tax.

In the early stages of your writing career you may not be earning anything at all, while at the same time you will be incurring expenses. This means you are working at a loss and you must record this loss against possible future earnings, and in order to prove this loss you must keep very careful records. Keep invoices for everything you buy, from biros and boxes of staples to film, cameras and office equipment.

Keep track of everything you spend on postage – this is a big expense for the freelance writer. Remember to get receipts for magazines and newspapers; I find it simpler to buy all my publications from one shop and pay the bill each month. Bus, train and taxi fares should all be recorded, as should the cost of air travel if used in the context of your travel writing.

In addition, keep copies of every query letter, covering letters accompanying manuscripts, and every rejection note you receive. These are proof of your intention to treat writing as a business and not just a hobby. If your intention is to earn income from your travel writing then any expenses incurred are tax deductible. You do not have to have sold your articles, only offered them for sale, to show your *intent*. You will probably never be asked to show your correspondence to the tax inspector, unless of course you submit a completely unbelievable tax return and your records are audited, but careful record keeping not only clarifies your tax situation but it is also the mark of a professional conducting his or her business in a proper manner. And business is what you are engaged in if you are writing for money.

Preparing your own tax return is not difficult, and many freelance writers do it, but if you prefer to hire an accountant, try to find one who understands writers and their circumstances. A good accountant can save you time and money and can advise you on such things as claiming a proportion of your home, heating and telephone bill against tax. You can do all this yourself too, of course, and there are Inland Revenue pamphlets printed which will advise you.

Editors' pet peeves – a checklist

I have tried to emphasise the importance of being professional in your approach to travel writing. Editors are not little gods whose every whim should be catered to, but they are busy people who work in a very competitive environment where they frequently receive many hundreds of submissions each week – so the easier you can make it for them to buy *your* travel article, the better for you.

Most of the following points have been covered already within the text of this book, but they bear repeating and I list below some of the things that make editors throw up their hands in despair. Use the following as a check list before you send out your travel article and in your dealings with editors and your chances of success will greatly increase.

Peeve No. 1: Articles that bear absolutely no relationship to the requirements of the magazine or newspaper they are submitted to. Remember, *marketing, marketing, marketing.*

Peeve No. 2: Messy manuscripts, with poor grammar and bad spelling.

Peeve No. 3: Unsolicited manuscripts sent in without a stamped, self-addressed envelope.

Peeve No. 4: Telephoning with half-formed ideas.

Peeve No. 5: Writers who ask editors for advice and helpful criticism.

Peeve No. 6: Telephoning a week after submitting the manuscript to see if the editor intends buying it.

Peeve No. 7: Not sticking to the required number of words.

Peeve No. 8: Failure to meet deadlines.

Counting words

Counting the number of words in your travel article can be very satisfying. It means you have finished the writing and, with some slight adjustment to bring it to the required number of words, you are ready to send it off.

From your market study, or from the editor if you have a commission, you will have an idea of the required length of the publication's travel articles. It is not a good idea to exceed this. No editor is going to quibble over a dozen or so words more or less, but they do like to know that you are aware of the desired length. Make a point of counting the number of words before you send off your article.

Most editors prefer to have an approximate word count typed on the upper right hand corner of the first page and the cover page. See Figures 7.1. and 7.2. Type the number of words in round figures, i.e. 1,500 words rather than 1,572 words.

A simple way to count the number of words in your article is as follows: count the words in ten lines and divide this figure by ten to give the number of words per line. Then count the number of lines in a full page, and multiply the words per line by the lines per page to arrive at the total number of words per page. Then all you have to do is multiply this number by the number of typed pages, allowing for illustrations if any.